SHINTO, SPIRITS, AND SHRINES:
RELIGION IN JAPAN

LUCENT LIBRARY *of* HISTORICAL ERAS

SHINTO, SPIRITS, AND SHRINES:
RELIGION IN JAPAN

SUZANNE SONNIER

LUCENT BOOKS

An imprint of Thomson Gale, a part of The Thomson Corporation

THOMSON

™

GALE

Detroit • New York • San Francisco • New Haven, Conn. • Waterville, Maine • London

LIBRARY OF CONGRESS CATALOGING-IN-PUBLICATION DATA

Sonnier, Suzanne.
  Shinto, Spirits, and Shrines : Religion in Japan / by Suzanne Sonnier.
    p. cm. -- (Lucent library of historical eras. Twentieth-century Japan)
  Includes bibliographical references and index.
  ISBN-13: 978-1-4205-0029-5 (hardcover)
  1. Shinto--Juvenile literature. I. Title.
  BL2220.S66 2007
  299.5'61--dc22

                                                        2007030621

ISBN-10: 1-4205-0029-5
Printed in the United States of America

Contents

Foreword

Looking back from the vantage point of the present, history can be viewed as a myriad of intertwining roads paved by human events. Some paths stand out—broad highways whose mileposts, even from a distance of centuries, are clear. The events that propelled the rise to power of Germany's Third Reich, its role in World War II, and its eventual demise, for example, are well defined and documented.

Other roads are less distinct, their route sometimes hidden from view. Modern legislatures may have developed from old tribal councils, for example, but the links between them are indistinct in places, open to discussion and interpretation.

The architecture of civilization—law, religion, art, science, and government—as well as the more everyday aspects of our culture—what we eat, what we wear—all developed along the historical roads and byways. In that progression can be traced every facet of modern life.

A broad look back along these roads reveals that many paths—though of vastly different character—seem to converge at a few critical junctions. These intersections are those great historical eras that echo over the long, steady course of human history, extending beyond the past and into the present.

These epic periods of time are the focus of Historical Eras. They shine through the mists of history like beacons, illuminated by a burst of creativity that propels events forward—so bright that we, from thousands of years away, can clearly see the chain of events leading to the present.

Each Historical Eras consists of a set of books that highlight various aspects of these major eras. For example, the Elizabethan England library features volumes on Queen Elizabeth I and her court, Elizabethan theater, the great playwrights, and everyday life in Elizabethan London.

The mini-library approach allows for the division of each era into its most significant and most interesting parts and the exploration of those parts in depth. Also, social and cultural trends as well as illustrative documents and eyewitness accounts can be prominently featured in individual volumes.

Historical Eras present a wealth of information to young readers. The lively narrative, fully documented primary and secondary source quotations, maps, photographs, sidebars, and annotated bibliographies serve as launching points for class discussion and further research.

In studying the great historical eras, students also develop a better understanding of our own times. What we learn from the past and how we apply it in the present may shape the future and may determine whether our era will be a guiding light to those traveling future roads.

Timeline

500s CE	Buddhism and Confucianism introduced to Japan	1926	Showa period begins
1600	Tokugawa period begins	1937	World War II begins
1854	Commodore Perry forcibly opens Japanese markets to the United States	1945	World War II ends; State Shinto ends
1868	Meiji era begins; Imperial Charter Oath created; policy to separate Buddhism from Shinto begins	1945–52	Allied occupation of Japan
1869	Yasukuni Shrine built	1946	Emperor Hirohito renounces his divinity; Association of Shinto Shrines formed
1870	The Great Teaching begins	1947	New Japanese Constitution enacted
1889	Imperial Constitution enacted	1978	Fourteen Class A war criminals enshrined at Yasukuni Shrine
1890	Imperial declaration on education	1989	Death of Emperor Hirohito; Emperor Akihito ascends the throne
1912	Taisho period begins		
1920	Meiji Shrine completed		

◆Introduction

A Blended Tradition

Religion is an important aspect of culture all over the world. A group's religious beliefs and practices help form its worldview. For the Japanese, religious practices are especially significant, as they help foster community values and unite society.

The native religion of Japan is Shinto. According to Shinto, there are many divine spirits in the world, called *kami*. Kami have a special connection to nature, so Japanese culture does as well.

Shinto does not have a doctrine that its followers must believe in to be part of the religion. Instead of focusing on beliefs, Shinto concentrates on practices. Therefore, performing rituals correctly is important. Many Shinto practices focus on common life events and protection of the community. Other rituals center on asking for personal benefits from the kami.

Although Shinto does not impose rules, it does promote certain behaviors and moral codes. The main principles of Shinto are outlined in what is known as the Four Affirmations. These endorse behaviors that show love of family, tradition, nature, purity, and kami.

Shinto is the original religion of Japan, but it is not the only influential religion. About 1500 years ago, Buddhism came to Japan. Many aspects of Buddhism were incorporated into the Japanese belief system.

Buddhists believe that people's own thoughts and behavior result in either their happiness or suffering. Buddhism offers the Four Noble Truths and the Eightfold Path to guide its followers. Buddhists believe they are reincarnated after death to live another life. By practicing the Buddha's teachings, one eventually attains complete peace and happiness and

Shinto festivals such as this one help create a sense of community.

is no longer reincarnated. Buddhist beliefs about the afterlife complement Shinto, which mostly focuses on life in this world. Buddhist funerals became the norm in Japan.

Another influential philosophy imported into Japan was Confucianism. Confucianism's concepts about ethics and morals were a significant addition to the Japanese belief system. Values such as the importance of education and levels of authority became prominent features of Japanese society.

For hundreds of years, Shinto and Buddhism grew and blended together in Japan. After centuries of mostly peaceful coexistence, however, some people began agitating to filter out foreign-based religions in favor of their native religion, Shinto. This movement, combined with other factors, helped lead to many changes in Japan. During the nineteenth century, the feudal system ended and the shoguns lost the right to rule the country. Japan's emperor was returned to power. The foundation for restoring imperial power was a new political philosophy called State Shinto.

According to ancient Shinto legend, the emperor descended directly from the highest of the kami, the sun goddess. State Shinto claimed that because of his divinity and historical continuity, the emperor rather than the shogunate should rule Japan. Government officials hoped that this decision would help unite Japan into a modern nation-state. Politicians of this era wanted to modernize Japan by adopting Western ideas for industry and economic growth. At the same time, they wished to retain Japan's uniqueness.

This movement led to the Meiji Restoration of 1868. Under the emperor, the state supported Shinto. The government discriminated against Buddhism, though many ordinary citizens retained some Buddhist beliefs and practices. Shinto shrines and priests were given state funding and put under the control of the government. All Japanese people had to register as parishioners at their local shrine.

The link between the emperor and Shinto was emphasized with nationwide teaching campaigns. The ultimate authority of the emperor was codified in the Imperial Constitution of 1889, which emphasized his special, divine status. It also promoted the idea that every citizen's first duty was toward the emperor and state.

The twentieth century saw a continuation of the nation-building strategies of State Shinto. Creation of a public education system made schooling mandatory. The schools were an important tool in conforming the nation's youth to the state's goals. New school-based rituals were created to venerate the emperor and other symbols of the nation. Required military service served a similar purpose while increasing the number of armed forces.

The new military might of Japan was evident in the early years of the 1900s. Japan went to war with several of its neighbors and successfully colonized new territory. Those who had died for Japan in these wars were honored by having their souls enshrined at Yasukuni Shrine.

Japan's military victories combined with extreme racism and nationalism in the 1920s and 1930s. The government emphasized Shinto legends to promote the idea that Japan was a superior nation with a divine destiny to expand its rule. This was a major factor in Japan's decision to attack the United States in World War II.

The Allied victory in that war led to the collapse of Japan's State Shinto. After the war, freedom of religion was introduced, and government and religion were officially separated. Emperor Hirohito renounced the idea of a divine emperor, which was a main belief of State Shinto. Though many officials were punished for their role in the war, the emperor was allowed to retain his title, though not his power. Although his role changed, the emperor is still an important symbol of heritage and tradition in Japan.

In other ways, too, Shinto and the government remain connected. For example, state officials continue to visit Yasukuni Shrine. Such visits stir debate and have become a lightning rod for differing versions of Japan's wartime aggression.

Just as the government and Shinto continue to be connected, so are the Japanese people and Shinto. Though most Japanese do not identify themselves as religious, elements of religion are clearly part of daily life in Japan. This is reflected, in part, in the Japanese focus on such values as selflessness and sustaining the welfare of the larger community.

Many people practice religious rites at home and in the community. Public festivals showcase certain rituals and practices. Festivals often include shrine visits and prayers. They emphasize the continuity of tradition and identity in Japan. In this way and others, Shinto was and continues to be a unifying force in Japan.

◆ Chapter One

The Japanese Way

The Japanese approach to religion is unique. In general, Japanese people practice an animistic form of religion. Animism is the belief that inanimate objects, such as trees and mountains, have souls. The natural world, therefore, is very important to the Japanese.

In Japan, religions are not mutually exclusive. Several philosophies and religions blend together. A Japanese person might practice two or more religions at the same time. Two belief systems, Shinto and Buddhism, are especially important. Shinto is the native religion of Japan. It focuses on the natural world and is generally life affirming. Buddhism came to Japan from China thousands of years ago. It has greatly contributed to Japanese religious life, especially concerning beliefs about death and the afterlife. A person may be both Shinto and Buddhist and feel no contradiction or conflict.

These two religions are compatible, in part, because they focus on different stages of the life cycle—Shinto on this life and Buddhism on the next life. This combination of philosophies creates a religious environment that makes Japan unique.

In Japan, religion is more about practice than belief. Japanese people focus on following ancient rituals and customs designed to meet specific goals, such as helping people lead a pure and balanced life. The Japanese are concerned with harmony, order, and the continuity of tradition, which allows them to pass values and practices from one generation to the next.

The Way of Buddha

Like Western religions, Buddhism can be traced to a founder. In the sixth and fifth centuries BCE, a man named Siddhartha

Comparative Religions Chart

	JUDAISM	CHRISTIANITY	ISLAM	HINDUISM	BUDDHISM
Prophet or Founder	Abraham	Jesus and his disciples	Mohammed	Has no founder	Siddhartha Gautama (a.k.a The Buddha)
Holy Book(s)	Torah Talmud	Bible (Old and New Testaments)	Q'uran	The Vedas The Bhagavad Gita	Tripitaka Sutras
Nature of deity	Only one god	One god who is a trinity of Father, Son, and Holy Spirit	Only one god	Single god that takes many forms	Many god-like beings
Purpose of Life	Live ethically	Achieve salvation through faith, sacraments, and/or good works	Earn a place in Paradise	Earn release from cycle of reincarnation by achieving enlightenment	• Avoid suffering • Achieve enlightenment • Reach nirvana
Afterlife	Not clearly defined but does acknowledge a next world	Heaven or Hell	Paradise or Hell	Reincarnation until enlightenment is achieved	Reincarnation until enlightenment is achieved and nirvana is reached
Practices	• Saturday Sabbath • Dietary laws forbid consumption of non-kosher foods • Holiday observances • Circumcision at birth • Bar/Bat Mitzvah in adolescence	• Prayer • Attendance at church • Holiday observances • Sunday Sabbath • Sacraments (in Catholicism)	• The Five Pillars: 1) Faith 2) Prayer 3) Alms 4) Pilgrimage (Hajj) 5) Fasting • Friday Sabbath • Dietary laws forbid consumption of alcohol and pig	• Yoga • Meditation • Pilgrimage to holy cities/sites • Devotion to god or goddess • Living according to one's purpose/role	• Meditation • Recitation of mantras

The Great Buddha of Kamakura, originally cast in bronze around 1252, is the second-largest Buddha statue in Japan.

of the altar. I knelt silently to say a prayer. Matsuda-san whispered to his wife's picture, "Cho-cho, it's Reido-san," just in case she had forgotten me.[4]

Reciprocity, or exchanging things for the benefit of both parties, is an important concept in Japanese society. Buddhism teaches that such exchanges exist between the living and the dead. The living care for their dead ancestors through rituals, and the dead reciprocate by watching over their living descendants.

Because of these beliefs and the fact that Shinto does not emphasize death and the afterlife, Japanese people often choose Buddhist rituals for their funerals. Most Japanese choose to be cremated with Buddhist rites. This tradition of cremation stems from the fact that the Buddha himself was cremated. Another common Japanese funeral ritual is moistening the deceased person's lips with water. This practice, like cremation, stems from events surrounding the death of the Buddha.

Though there are far more Buddhist cemeteries in Japan than Shinto cemeteries, a small minority of Japanese do choose to have Shinto funerals. An important example is the imperial family of Japan. A special Shinto cemetery in Tokyo is the final resting place for emperors and their family members.

Several different branches of Buddhism exist in Japan today. Of these, Zen Buddhism is one of the most popular. Zen Buddhism came to Japan from China in the twelfth century. Zen emphasizes the quest for self-enlightenment through self-lessness, discipline, and meditation.

The Japanese tea ceremony was inspired by Zen and emphasizes its Buddhist ideals. It has been an important part of Japanese culture for centuries and can still be enjoyed today. The ceremony is highly symbolic and ritualized. In his work *The Book of Tea*, Kakuzo Okakura writes:

Tea began as a medicine and grew into a beverage. In China, in the eighth century, it entered the realm of poetry as one of the polite amusements. The fifteenth century saw Japan enable it into a religion… Teaism. Teaism is a cult founded on the adoration of the beautiful among the sordid facts of everyday existence. … It is essentially a worship of the Imperfect, as it is a tender attempt to accomplish something possible in this impossible thing we know as life.

It is hygiene, for it enforces cleanliness; it is economics, for it shows comfort in simplicity rather than in the complex and costly; it is moral geometry, inasmuch as it defines our sense of proportion to the universe. It represents the true spirit of Eastern democracy by making all its [practitioners] aristocrats in taste.[5]

A formal tea ceremony can last for as long as four hours. Tea drinking was introduced to Japan in the 9th century.

The Way of Kami

Shinto is an ancient religion native to Japan. In Japanese, it is called *kami no michi* (the way of the kami), referring to the deities, or spirits, that form the center of Shinto belief. The religion has no single founder or figure of worship. It did not even have a name before Buddhism reached Japan. To distinguish between the ancient religion and the Way of Buddha, native Japanese practices were labeled "the Divine Way," pronounced in Chinese as *Shin-tao*.

Shinto teaches that humans and spirits exist together in the world. Shinto acknowledges nature as the divine power in the universe because the Shinto deities —the kami—reside in nature.

For thousands of years, Shinto has been the basis for the Japanese way of life. It embodies the customs and traditions of Japan. While Japanese Buddhism focuses on the afterlife, Shinto focuses on the world of the living. Shinto rituals are centered on life transitions, such as marriage and childbirth, as well as maintaining good fortune and health.

Like Buddhism, Shinto endorses certain behaviors. These behaviors are governed by Shinto's guiding principles, which are called the Four Affirmations. An affirmation is a positive attitude about or action toward something. The Four Affirmations of Shinto are: honoring the family and Japanese tradition and customs; loving nature; having purity, or personal cleanliness; and worshiping the kami. These affirmations are central to Japanese culture and help guide the Japanese in the conduct of their daily lives.

The Japanese connection to the natural world is particularly strong. Many scholars believe that Shinto arose in prehistoric times from nature cults. Historian Sir George Sansom believed that these cults resulted from the awe of prehistoric immigrants arriving in Japan:

> It may be that… the genial [friendly] climate of Japan, with its [abundance] of trees and flowering shrubs, its fertile soil, and its wealth of running streams, was so pleasing as to make upon them a profound [strong] impression, stored up in the racial consciousness as a pervading [deep] sense of gratitude. Certainly their religion was … a religion of love and gratitude rather than of fear, and the purpose of their religious rites was to praise and thank as much as to placate [satisfy] and mollify [calm] their divinities [spirits]. The very names given in their mythology to their country—… the Land of Fresh Rice Ears of a Thousand Autumns—and to their gods—the Princess Blooming Like the Flowers of the Trees …—testify to their strong sense of the beauty and richness of their environment.[6]

Kami

Millions of kami are honored in Japan. Belief in kami reinforces Shintoists' reverence toward nature. The kami reside in natural objects such as mountains, rivers, lakes, and rocks. They hold and direct the power of nature. These spirits favor purity and cleanliness and emphasize harmony and happiness.

In Japanese, the word *kami* means "that which is hidden," and its true meaning is difficult to grasp. Unlike supreme beings such as gods, kami are not perfect or all-powerful. A kami can be a spirit that resides in a person or natural object, such as a plant. It can be a natural force, such as a storm. Kami can also be places or ancestors.

Shinto views the world as a good and positive place, and kami are available to people to help make their lives happy. Like human beings, however, kami are not always virtuous. They can cause trouble and are the source of suffering such as sickness, natural disaster, and failure. The Japanese do not classify kami as good or evil. Instead, kami may behave roughly or gently, according to the circumstances. A kami that behaves roughly one day by sending a typhoon may behave gently later when it sends much-needed rain for dying crops.

Shintoists believe that the kami of their ancestors gather in natural places, particularly in the mountains. Mount Fuji is thought to be a kami and is the most sacred natural place in Japan, in part because of its appearance. Travel writer Susan Orlean describes Mount Fuji as being "so pretty and so weirdly symmetrical that people have always believed it was supernatural and sanctified."[7]

The Divine Wind

In the thirteenth century, Japan was a peaceful, prosperous place. Military rule and the development of the samurai class had brought order after years of civil war. While Japan had been fighting its civil war, the Mongols, a people from North-Central Asia, conquered China and Korea. By the time Japan achieved peace, the Mongols were looking to expand their rule to the Japanese islands.

In 1281, the Mongol emperor Kublai Khan sent a fleet across the East China Sea to attack Japan. The ships never arrived. They were destroyed by a typhoon that lasted for two days. The Japanese interpreted the typhoon as an act of kami and as a sign that their land was protected by the gods. They called the typhoon *kamikaze* (divine wind).

Centuries later, during World War II, the Japanese military sought to protect Japan with its own divine wind—pilots who flew planes loaded with explosives into U.S. warships. Today, we continue to refer to those pilots as kamikaze.

Many Shinto shrines are located in natural settings throughout Japan. Historian C. Scott Littleton writes:

In addition to mountains, countless other natural features are held to be sacred. Indeed, almost every distinctive rock outcrop, river, hill, and waterfall is likely to have some association with a local temple, shrine, or both. Examples include the magnificent Nachi waterfall in Wakayama prefecture and a spectacular waterfall in Akita, Honshu, both of which, like Fuji-san, are widely conceived to be powerful kami—deities in their own right—and therefore offer propitious places for worshipers to parade with a *mikoshi* [a portable shrine].[8]

The role of kami is a good example of the blending of Shinto and Buddhist beliefs. Shintoists believe buddhas are kami; Buddhists accept kami as spirits of buddhas. In many Japanese homes, the Buddha is honored at a family altar and kami are honored at the *kamidana* (a family shrine).

The Purpose of Worship

Worship has a dual purpose in almost every religion: to ask for benefits in the living world, such as material goods, and

Mount Fuji, Japan's highest mountain, is held by many to be sacred. Some believe the dormant volcano is home to Shinto goddess Konoha Nasakuya-Hime.

to ask for benefits in the spiritual world, such as a high status in the afterlife. Many Japanese turn to Buddhism for their concerns about the afterlife. Because Shinto beliefs focus on the living world, many Japanese pray to kami as a means of improving their lives in the present.

Shintoists offer devotion and money to kami, and kami are expected to reciprocate with practical benefits that the worshiper can use. The benefit expected depends on which kami is being asked. Different deities can provide different benefits, such as a good harvest or success in business. Many worshipers ask for nonmaterial benefits, such as good health or a happy marriage.

Shintoists believe that prayer and worship are an important part of daily life. These acts acknowledge that people cannot do everything for themselves. Devotion is not only asking for benefits, but it is also a declaration that worshipers believe and will lead good lives. Praying to kami and buddhas establishes a partnership with them, which leads the believer to a deeper faith and peace of mind. Historians Ian Reader and George J. Tanabe Jr. write:

Some figures of worship can readily straddle the borders between Buddhism and Shinto, but even if they do not, their importance is related more to their reputation in providing benefits than to their identification with a specific religious tradition. Moreover, those who pray for benefits do not normally limit themselves to praying within the boundaries of one religious tradition but seek according to their needs: in this sense, there are no borders between religions. Rather, there are differentiations between types of benefit and the efficacy through which they can be met.[9]

Shinto Shrines

Shrines are found throughout Japan. A kamidana, or household shrine, exists in most traditional Japanese homes. The shrine holds the names of ancestral kami and the traditional mirror that indicates the presence of the kami. Because kami must be nourished to function well, someone in the home tends the kamidana daily. Small cups of *sake* (rice wine), food, water, and salt are offered fresh each day, along with an evergreen twig. The family prays to the kami for blessings and benefits for members of the household. Noriko Nomura describes her family's kamidana:

Kamidanas, or household shrines, are usually positioned to face east or south.

It is a wooden shelf. We keep a special piece of paper on the shelf. On the paper is the name of a Kami. This Kami may be an ancestor, or it may be another Kami. Sometimes we put a branch of evergreen there too. The evergreen stands for long life. In the morning my mother and I place a bowl of rice and water on the Kami Dama for the Kami. These are offerings to show that we honor the Kami.[10]

Every town has at least one shrine honoring its guardian kami. Most shrines are located in beautiful places that promote harmony among nature, humans, and kami. The Japanese build Shinto shrines in areas not simply because they are beautiful, however, but because people believe that kami are there. Some places are sacred because certain kami temporarily live there. Shrines are constructed in that area to worship that kami. A sacred space is set apart for the kami, which comes when summoned and then leaves again.

Shrines range from large and permanent to small and portable. Shinto priests typically care for large shrines, such as the one found at Mount Fuji. Japanese people often look after small shrines. Local shrines are owned and cared for by everyone within a community. Caretakers give offerings of food and make sure the shrine is maintained properly for worship and celebrations.

Most Shinto shrines have a standard structure. A *torii* (gate) is at the entrance. A stone trough provides clean water to wash with before entering the presence of the kami. Cleansing is essential to worship, as kami favor cleanliness and orderliness. People are expected to wash their hands and rinse their mouth with water and salt. When worshipers enter a shrine, they leave behind the impure outside world and enter the pure, everlasting world of the kami. As one book explains, "in the West we have the saying that 'cleanliness is next to godliness' but the Japanese conception may be closer to 'cleanliness is not distinct from godliness.'"[11]

Another feature of a Shinto shrine is a building in which people make offerings and pray. A second building houses images of kami and is used only by priests. Some large shrines include many buildings grouped together in a complex. These structures may house administrative offices and theaters. Some shrine complexes are surrounded by a fence and have many torii. They may include a fountain to provide water for purification.

Before entering a shrine, a visitor or priest rings a bell or claps to alert the kami to the presence of a human. After cleansing, the worshiper makes an offering of money to the kami and then goes to a building to honor the kami and ask for benefits. The kami is not depicted by an image, but by a mirror that represents its presence. This is in accordance with the legend of Amaterasu, the sun goddess, who left behind a mirror to represent her existence when she had gone.

The most sacred Shinto shrine in Japan is Ise, the shrine to the sun goddess

The floating torii mark the entrance to the Itsukushima Shrine on the island of Honshu, Miya-jima. Built in 593 AD, it is one of the most photographed sites in Japan.

26   Shinto, Spirits, and Shrines: Religion in Japan

The Land of the Rising Sun

According to Shinto belief, Japan was created by two kami named Izanagi and Izanami. Standing on a rainbow, Izanagi and Izanami dipped a spear into the ocean. The first drop of water from the tip of the spear created the first Japanese island. Izanagi and Izanami then stood on that first island and created the rest of Japan's archipelago, or group of islands.

Izanagi and Izanami gave birth to more kami. These offspring kami became gods of nature such as the wind, trees, mountains, and rain. Thus, Izanagi and Izanami are considered the parents to all of Japan's geography.

One of Izanagi and Izanami's children, Amaterasu, seemed brighter and more beautiful than the rest. They placed her in the sky and made her the sun goddess, the highest of the heavenly kami and the most supreme of all kami. Amaterasu is considered the beginning of Japan's royal family. According to legend, Japan's first emperor, Jimmu Tenno, was Amaterasu's great-great-great-grandson. In honor of Amaterasu, Japan is called the Land of the Rising Sun.

A hanging scroll by Kobayashi Eitaku (1843–1890) called "Izanagi and Izanami Creating the Japanese Islands," is displayed in the Museum of Fine Arts, Boston.

Amaterasu. This large complex has an outer shrine and an inner shrine, each with several outer buildings. Both shrines are built in traditional Japanese style, made completely out of wood. Every twenty years, they are torn down and rebuilt nearby exactly as before. This is believed to renew the life and energy of

Prime Minister Koizumi Junichiro visits the Ise Shrine on January 4, 2006. It is customary for the Japanese prime minister to visit the shrine at the beginning of the new year.

the kami. The site of the previous complex is covered with white pebbles.

Few shrines are built in strictly Japanese style today. Early Buddhists believed that kami, much like humans, were in their present state because of their karma. Buddhists established temples near Shinto shrines to help kami and humans understand the causes of suffering and the way to end the cycle of life, death, and rebirth. The grander Chinese structural style and colors such as red and gold of these Buddhist temples were incorporated into Shinto shrines, which become more

The Kamigamo Shrine, originally built in the 7th century, is the oldest Shinto shrine in Kyoto. It was declared a World Heritage Site in 1994.

detailed. Some torii became elaborate gates with many posts. Simple roofs became pagodas with sweeping curves. This blending of architectural styles is another example of how Japan created its own unique religious tradition by blending Shinto and Buddhism.

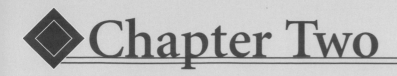

◆ Chapter Two

Shinto Helps Unite Japan

Shinto is important to Japanese history for both religious and political reasons. Beginning in the nineteenth century, some Japanese scholars started to believe that Shinto could and should be separated from Buddhist influences. This development helped spark a movement that would change the religious and political systems of Japan. This movement resulted in the Meiji Restoration of 1868.

Under this new political system, Japanese government came under a central authority. The emperor, who was granted divine status, became ruler. The foundation of this system was the political philosophy called State Shinto. This system used Shinto beliefs blended with elements of the Chinese philosophy of Confucianism to create a monarchy based on religion. While this system resembled the governing styles of Western European nations, the blending of Shinto with politics gave the system a uniquely Japanese flavor. In this way, Japanese leaders used Shinto as an institution to help unify the people and move the country into the modern world. Before State Shinto came into play, however, a series of events occurred to set the stage for major change throughout Japan.

The End of an Era

The years from 1600 to 1868 are known as the Tokugawa, or Edo, period in Japan. Tokugawa was the family name of powerful shoguns, military generals who ruled the country. The city of Edo, later called Tokyo, was the seat of their power. Although Japan's emperor and imperial family existed at this time, they occupied a mostly symbolic role.

During the Tokugawa era, Japan experienced an unusually peaceful time. All was not well, however. One problem was that the shoguns had isolated Japan from the rest of the world. Within the nation, natural disasters, famine, and the wearing away of strict levels of authority led to suffering and unease among the people. From without, European and, later, American forces pressured the government. They forced it to agree to trade deals that were unfavorable to Japan.

Some Japanese viewed increased exposure to Western culture and industry as a threat. Others resented the feudal-like rule of the Tokugawa. This feeling was aggravated when it became clear in the 1850s that the shoguns would not be able to protect Japan from invasion by Western forces. A fleet of U.S. warships appeared in Japanese waters to turn back the tide of Japan's isolation and open

Japan to trade. After this, a movement proposing that the emperor be returned to rule began to gain ground.

A Return to Cultural Roots

Because of these concerns, some Japanese sought a change in leadership. One important element driving this desire was the Kokugaku, or national learning, movement. National learning began to be discussed in the 1600s and 1700s. Historian Helen Hardacre notes that the movement's leaders wanted to end what they considered the polluting of pure, ancient Japanese culture by Western influences and by Buddhism. She writes that "Buddhism was attacked as the

The Black Ships

Beginning in 1641, the Tokugawa employed a policy of *sokoku*, meaning "lock-up of country." Japanese people were not allowed to leave the country and foreigners were not allowed to enter. This strategy aimed to tightly control Japan's culture and commerce. The government sought to limit the spread of Christianity as well. This religion had been introduced by Westerners, and it was believed to be a disruptive influence. Only limited trade was allowed in certain areas of Japan with the Dutch, Chinese, and Koreans.

This policy of isolation was ended by the dramatic 1853 landing in Edo Bay of

ships known as the Black Fleet. The fleet was commanded by Commodore Matthew C. Perry of the United States. The nickname of the fleet derived from either the hull color, made black by waterproofing tar, or by the color of the smoke from the coal-burning ships. The Japanese were amazed and intimidated by these four modern warships.

Perry had come to open trade with Japan, using force if necessary. On a second trip in 1854, Perry persuaded the Japanese government to sign a treaty. This document established formal governmental and trade relations with the United States.

agency most to blame for Japan's loss of its original way of life."[12]

In order to return Japan to its roots, Kokugaku scholars rejected the study of Chinese and Buddhist teachings. They turned to ancient Japanese literary works, such as the *Kojiki, Nihongi,* and *Man'yoshu,* written in the eighth century. These texts include stories and poems describing the creation of the kami and their relation to the imperial family. The following tale from the *Nihongi* depicts some of the deeds of Jimmu Tenno. This legendary conqueror reportedly descended from the sun goddess Amaterasu. He became Japan's first emperor, from whom all following emperors descended.

The Emperor Kami Yamato Iharebiko's personal name was Hikohoho-demi [later known as Jimmu Tenno]. … From his birth, this Emperor was of clear intelligence and resolute [determined] will. At the age of 15 he was made heir to the throne. When he grew up, he married Ahira-tsu-hime … and by her he had Tagishi-mimi no Mikoto and Kisu-mimi no Mikoto.

When he reached the age of 45, he addressed his elder brothers and his children, saying: "Of old, our Heavenly [gods] … pointing to this land of fair rice-ears of the fertile reed-plain, gave it to our Heavenly ancestor. … [Then our ancestor], throwing open the barrier of Heaven and clearing a cloud-path, urged on his

superhuman course until he came to rest. At this time the world was given over to widespread desolation [unhappiness]. It was an age of darkness and disorder. In this gloom, therefore, be fostered justice. … Our Imperial ancestors and Imperial parent, like gods, like sages, accumulated happiness and amassed glory. Many years elapsed. From the date when our Heavenly ancestor descended until now it is over 1,792,470 years. But the remote regions do not yet enjoy the blessings of Imperial rule. Every town has always been allowed to have its lord, and every village its chief, who, each one for himself, makes division of territory and practices mutual aggression and conflict."[13]

Enlightened Rule

Inspired by the lessons of the national learning movement and feeling betrayed by the Tokugawa's dealings with the West, a group of warriors overthrew the shogun in 1868. They reestablished the emperor as the chief political figure in Japanese government.

The emperor restored to power inherited his position while still a teenager. Given the name Mutsuhito at birth, he adopted the name Meiji, which means "enlightened rule," when he became emperor. From early in his reign, many reforms were begun in Japan. The first major change was the introduction of the

According to Japanese tradition, Emperor Jimmu (660 BCE–585 BCE) was the founder of Japan's imperial dynasty. Jimmu defeated many chieftans to unite the regions of Japan under his rule.

Imperial Charter Oath of 1868. This document promised to modernize Japan and included new opportunities for democratic participation in government.

While the emperor was the head of the government in title, he actually exerted little power in the early years of his reign. His advisors, who were members of the group that had overthrown the Tokugawa, ran the government. They mostly used the emperor's influence to justify their actions. In a different way, though, the emperor was a central piece of the new political system. As Meiji leaders were modernizing Japan's economy and social structure, they resurrected the notion of the emperor as a divine figure. As a result, he became a powerful symbol of Japanese culture and history.

Through all these changes, the Meiji leaders sought to move Japan into the modern era while retaining a strong symbol of leadership from the past. These reformers declared Shinto, rather than Buddhism, to be Japan's national religion. According to scholars at Columbia University, "by associating Shinto with the imperial line, which reached back into legendary times, Japan had not only the oldest ruling house in the world, but a powerful symbol of age-old national unity."[14]

The Shinto Way

Supporters of national learning and the new government wanted to solidify Japanese unity by introducing a new way of thinking about religion, and about

Emperor Meiji, who was born Prince Mutsuhito in 1852, served as Japan's 122nd emperor from 1867 until his death in 1912.

Shinto in particular.

Prior to the Meiji period, people rarely thought of religion as something separate from their everyday existence. Shinto was woven into the fabric of life the way we might think of seeing, eating, or celebrating as a part of life. Shinto was not something people brought into their lives from the outside, but rather a natural, integrated way of honoring the internal spirit or nature of life itself. Promoting or advertising Shinto had not occurred to people. In fact, prior to the national learning movement, the Japanese rarely even used the word *Shinto* in conversation.

Japanese people worshipped various Shinto kami at public shrines. They did

The Imperial Charter Oath

The Meiji leaders wrote the Imperial Charter Oath of 1868, which aimed to establish a broad base of civil rights, services, and national goals and to create a framework for a constitution and laws. It laid out five areas for change:

- Deliberative assemblies (debate groups) shall be widely established and all matters decided by public discussion.
- All classes, high and low, shall unite in vigorously carrying out the administration of affairs of state.
- The common people, no less than the civil and military officials, shall each be allowed to pursue his own calling so that there may be no discontent.
- Evil customs of the past shall be broken off and everything based upon the just laws of nature.
- Knowledge shall be sought throughout the world so as to strengthen the foundations of imperial rule.[1]

[1]Ryusaku Tsunoda, Wm. Theodore de Bary, and Donald Keene, comp., *Sources of Japanese Tradition*, volume II (New York: Columbia University Press, 1958), 137, http://www. indiana. edu/~hisdcl/h207_2002/meijiconstitution.htm (accessed April 16, 2007).

not, however, think of themselves as being part of a particular religion called Shinto. Priests of the Tokugawa period tended to kami shrines and performed Shinto rituals, but they did not consider Shinto a specific religion. Hardacre writes that

> priests had little sense of being involved in a common undertaking that could appropriately be named with a single term. Probably no one but priests devoted to National Learning regarded themselves as exclusively Shintoist, in the sense of being entirely independent of Buddhism, and not even they used the word Shinto exclusively. Thus the idea of Shinto as an independ-

ent religion scarcely existed before the Meiji Restoration.[15]

The Creation of State Shinto

The new Meiji leaders decided to create a new version of Shinto, called State Shinto. They believed that if the people viewed Shinto as a uniquely Japanese religion, headed by the emperor and the government, it would help unify Japan into a modern state. Toward this end, the leaders created a Department of Divinity. This department had authority over all religious affairs throughout Japan.

The government carried out its new Shinto policy through various means.

National leaders organized a system under which they controlled formerly independent Shinto shrines to special deities, or gods. The Ise Shrine stood at the top of the hierarchy. The sun goddess Amaterasu was worshipped at Ise. This served to remind the Japanese people of the divine origins of the emperor.

In a break with custom, the emperor began to perform many religious rites that were treated as national holidays. In the 1870s, a new annual calendar was created to mark these celebrations. Some of the rites recalled Emperor Jimmu's founding of the imperial dynasty, Emperor Jimmu's death, and the celebration of Emperor Meiji's birthday. Other rites honored the imperial ancestors and major deities. Still others celebrated the importance of the harvest, in particular the rice harvest.

A New Constitution Promotes the Emperor

The 1889 Constitution of the Empire of Japan addressed the ancient and divine ancestral line of the emperor and the emperor's importance to the state. The preamble, or introduction, to the document glorifies the emperor and his ancestors, referring to their kindness and protection. It reminds the people that the imperial line has been "unbroken for ages eternal" and that its desire has always been "to promote the welfare and development of the moral and intellectual qualities of the beloved subjects." It further points out that the constitution will "exhibit the principles by which the people are to be guided in their conduct and are forever to conform."[16]

The preamble and constitution leave no uncertainty about who is in charge—the emperor and his descendants—and claim the imperial line's right to use its authority. The first chapter of the constitution deals with the emperor's role, with one article stating "the Emperor is sacred and inviolable [untouchable]."[17] The constitution also laid out the many powers accorded to the emperor, including his command of the military. It further stated that only the emperor or his advisors could amend, or change, the laws.

The constitution, which remained the basic document of Japanese law from 1889 until 1947, reinforced the Meiji idea that the emperor was both the high priest of Shinto and a godlike leader. Citizens now had both a religious and a civic duty to worship and obey the emperor.

Another tool that underlined the relationship between the emperor and the nation was the new national anthem. Prior to 1868, Japan had no national anthem. John William Fenton, a British military bandleader who worked in Japan, suggested the necessity of creating one. The words of the song are from a tenth-century Japanese poem. The English translation reads, "May the reign of the Emperor continue for a thousand, nay, eight thousand generations and for the eternity that it takes for small pebbles to grow into a great rock and become covered with moss."[18]

Purifying Shinto

To aid the spread of State Shinto, the government sought to purify Shinto by ridding it of foreign influences. This meant eliminating elements of Buddhism from Shinto. In 1868, officials announced the policy of *shinbutsu bunri* (separation of kami from Buddhism). Such a separation would not be easy. Shinto and Buddhism had blended for more than a thousand years. The Japanese revered Buddhas as kami, and most people practiced some form of Buddhism along with Shinto.

Outwardly, Shinto's separateness could be partially accomplished with relative ease. For example, Shinto objects were to be removed from Buddhist temples and Buddhist objects were to be removed from Shinto shrines. Additionally, leaders offered Shinto funerals as the alternative to traditional Buddhist funerals.

Complete separation of the two practices proved far more difficult to achieve. Buddhism deeply influenced Shinto, and its elements were popular. Many Japanese people were attached to Buddhist beliefs and rituals and were reluctant to abandon them.

To Shinto priests, State Shinto came as welcome news. Under its policies, they became public servants, and the government began to fund important shrines. For many years, priests lacked formal recognition or support for their role in

Shinto. Some of them now took advantage of their new position and vented their frustration in violent ways. According to Hardacre, "the order for the separation of Buddhism and Shinto was accompanied by the unauthorized plun-

Waka Poetry

Waka is a traditional Japanese poetic form. Also known as *tanka*, this type of Japanese poetry dates from at least the eighth century. Many members of the imperial family wrote waka, which is said to be expressive in a uniquely Japanese way. Emperor Meiji and his wife, Empress Shoken, composed thousands of waka poems, including the following:

> For the times to come
> And of meeting what must be met
> All of our people
> Must be taught to walk along
> The path of sincerity
> (Emperor Meiji)

> Every morning
> We gaze into our mirrors
> Which are unblemished;
> Oh, that we could attain
> Such a purity of soul
> (Empress Shoken)[1]

[1]"Waka," Meiji Shrine, http://www.meijijingu.or.jp/english/intro/waka/index.htm (accessed April 16, 2007).

dering of everything Buddhist in which the pent-up resentment of the Shinto priesthood was unleashed in ferocious, [vengeful] destruction."[19]

The Shinto priests, with the support of the government, stripped the Buddhist priests of their authority, land, and goods. They created weapons from Buddhist statues and tools used in religious ceremonies.

Some Buddhist priests were jailed; others were executed. One such priest was Ishikawa Tairei, who was beheaded for his role in an 1871 uprising that protested the new policies. Tairei related the following:

> I was led through town in shackles and taken [from the jail] to the courthouse [for further questioning]. All along the streets, great crowds of people had gathered to watch. It is so strange. I have no desire for fame or profit, I merely seek to live within my religion; within my heart there is no shame. Ahh! Who understands my true intention? The Buddha? The Kami? Why do the common people fail to understand? Laugh if you will! Slander me if you will! Those who laugh are but the enemies of the Buddha. Slanderers are but the enemies of the dharma [truth].[20]

For its part, the government blamed the Buddhist priests for their own downfall, calling them ignorant, confused, and impure.

Throughout the Meiji era, official persecution of Buddhism came and went. Buddhist rituals were deeply ingrained in Japanese traditions. Regardless of the government's position, many average Japanese people continued to engage in Buddhist rites and beliefs.

The Great Teaching

In an attempt to hasten the end of Buddhist influences, the government began an educational campaign. Repelling the spread of Christianity and promoting official State Shinto doctrine were its other aims. This campaign, which took place from 1870 to 1884, was called the Great Teaching. The program had three main elements: the Three Great Teachings, the Great Teaching Institute, and the national evangelists.

The Three Great Teachings were the government's authorized doctrine. They laid out the main lessons the government wanted the Japanese people to follow. These were: respect for the gods and love of country; making clear the principles of Heaven and the Way of Man; and reverence for the emperor and obedience to the will of the court.

The Three Great Teachings reflect both Shinto and Confucian themes. Although Confucianism was not native to Japan, but rather imported from China, its

The philosophy of Confucius (ca. 551 BCE—ca. 479 BCE) emphasizes morality, justice and sincerity.

teachings had been sowed into Japanese society for hundreds of years.

Confucianism taught that everyone has a role to fill based on his or her place in the family and in society. It said that people have a duty to fulfill their role and always act in an ethical way. Confucianism emphasized values such as honesty and loyalty. The government saw special value in the idea that authority, ritual, and ethical behavior were good ways to achieve social order. Historian Richard Hooker writes that

Confucius had one overwhelming message: if we are to achieve a state of orderliness and peace, we need to return to traditional values of virtue. These values are based entirely on one concept: *jen*, which is best translated as "humaneness," but can also mean "humanity," "benevolence," "goodness," or "virtue." This humaneness is a [somewhat] strange concept to Western eyes, because it is not primarily a [usable] virtue. ... Like his contemporaries, Confucius believed that the human order in some way reflected the divine order, or the patterns of heaven.[21]

The Great Teaching Institute was a school formed to train people to become instructors of the Three Great Teachings. These instructors were called national evangelists (missionaries). Other schools with a similar purpose were located throughout the country. Many Shinto and even Buddhist priests became national evangelists. Thousands of them spread the Three Great Teachings throughout Japan. Along with these, they taught that there was virtue in paying taxes, as well as being drafted to serve in the military. The evangelists supported mandatory (required) education, the solar calendar, military buildup, and "the [introduction] of Western knowledge and culture."[22] The messages of the national evangelists provide another example of how the government used State Shinto for its purposes.

Some Japanese resisted the new order and made their feelings known. They wrote forceful letters to newspapers, describing State Shinto in negative terms. Hardacre notes that people "[made fun of] the campaign mercilessly, complaining that the evangelists' internal rivalries were more likely to drive the [people] to Christianity than to prevent its advance."[23] Continuing to describe the content of the public's letters, Hardacre relates, "No one likes Shinto funerals, they complain; the teachings are not believable; the sermons are boring; the evangelists are ridiculous and unfit to serve the nation; Shinto priests are ritualists—it is absurd to have them teaching a creed [set of religious beliefs]; Shinto has nothing to contribute to ethical thought."[24]

Eventually, however, the Great Teaching campaign succeeded in many ways. It created a broad awareness of Shinto as separate from Buddhism. It effectively educated the people about State Shinto. Additionally, it helped the broader governmental goals of modernizing Japan and unifying the people.

In these ways and others, the Meiji era was a time of great transformation for Japan. Many of the changes had to do with Shinto, either directly or indirectly. During this period, the definition and uses of Shinto were altered to support the government's goals. In the pre-Meiji period, Shinto was mostly focused on local shrines dedicated to kami. By the end of the period, Shinto was centered on allegiance to Japan and its emperor. When Emperor Meiji died in 1912, the people mourned him greatly. State Shinto had changed the nature of religious worship in Japan and had a great impact on the future of the country.

Chapter Three

Shinto and the Second World War

As the twentieth century progressed, ideas surrounding religion became increasingly important to Japan's national and foreign policies. Japanese politicians and others used State Shinto to justify their goals. These goals eventually collided with those of the West and resulted in World War II.

State Shinto advanced through many avenues. The government used the national educational system to teach its point of view to the nation's youth. Students were taught about the divinity of the emperor and the superiority of Japanese culture. The government's policy of imperialism was linked to State Shinto in many ways as well. Belief in Japanese superiority fed the desire for conquest and was used to rationalize the brutal treatment of conquered peoples. Additionally, the shrine system proved to be an important medium for state-authorized religion.

Teaching State Values

Education has been important to the Japanese for centuries. This is partly due to Confucian ideas that were absorbed into the Japanese value system. Confucius advocated educating all people, regardless of wealth or social class.

Prior to 1868, thousands of temple schools existed in Japan. There, students learned subjects such as reading, writing, math, and calligraphy (artistic handwriting). The Meiji government changed the school system when it instituted education reform in 1872. The government created a public school system and required all children to attend elementary school. This reform was very successful. By the turn of the century, more than 90 percent of school-age children were enrolled in elementary school. Because of this, Japan's literacy rate, or ability to read and write, was exceptionally high.

Confucius and Education

Confucian principles are woven throughout Japanese society. This poem by a Chinese emperor emphasizes the Confucian belief in the importance of education:

> To enrich your family, there is no need to buy good land:
> Books hold a thousand measures of grain.
> For an easy life, there is no need to build mansion:
> In books are found houses of gold.
> When you go out, do not be upset if no one follows you:

> In books there will be a crowd of horses and carriages.
> If you wish to marry, don't be upset if you don't have a go-between:
> In books there are girls with faces like jade.
> A young man who wishes to be somebody
> Will devote his time to the Classics.
> He will face the window and read.[1]

[1] "Confucianism and the Chinese Scholastic System," http://www. csupomona.edu /~plin/ls201/confucian2.html (accessed May 4, 2007).

Officials believed that education was a virtue unto itself, but they knew that education could enhance State Shinto. They used the education system to further such goals as modernizing the nation and bringing government under a central power. To this end, students studied subjects such as reading and writing and learned the importance of levels of authority, loyalty to the emperor, and morality. Shinto priests often served as public school teachers. Shinto shrines were a popular destination for school trips. The educational curriculum reflected the state's desire to become stronger to compete with the West, but in a uniquely Japanese way.

Rules for Behavior

The Imperial Rescript on Education of 1890 made the state's wishes clear. It praised Japan and its people for their historically deep and "everlasting" virtue, loyalty, and piety. It went on to say that these traits represented Japan's "fundamental character" and were the foundation for its education. The document further specified how people should behave:

> Know Ye, Our subjects, be filial [dutiful] to your parents, affectionate to your brothers and sisters; as husbands and wives be harmonious, as friends true; bear yourselves in modesty and moderation; extend your

By 1949, Japanese students were once again filling large classrooms.

benevolence [kindness] to all; pursue learning and cultivate arts, and thereby develop intellectual faculties and perfect moral powers; furthermore advance public good and promote common interests; always respect the Constitution and observe the laws; should emergency arise, offer yourselves courageously to the state; and thus guard and maintain the prosperity of Our Imperial Throne. …

The 30th day of the 10th month of the 23rd year of Meiji. (Imperial Sign Manual. Imperial Seal)[25]

The document said Japan's imperial ancestors taught these "infallible [flawless] … and true" values and that they would continue to be taught. This document became central to the goals of State Shinto. In it, students were reminded that the emperor had divine origins and that the Japanese were one people. Above all, it made clear that people had a duty to serve the state.

All schools displayed the document and all schoolchildren memorized it. Many schools built shrines to house this document along with the official photograph of the emperor. New customs dictated how the rescript was to be treated. These included requiring teachers, students, area residents, and local officials to parade the document to the school. Then they had to set up a special place where the text would be read and make an offering of rice cakes.

The Empire Expands

By the late nineteenth century, many State Shinto goals were gaining ground. The government was centralizing, education and the military were modernizing, and the economy was industrializing. Many Japanese people were seeing themselves as part of a special nation, centered on its emperor. A strong sense of nationalism arose.

At the same time, Japan grew worried about its position in Asia. It was concerned about maintaining its influence in the region and afraid of being conquered by Western powers. This fate had already befallen some other Asian nations. In response, the government updated and expanded the military. Compulsory conscription laws meant that every man was required to serve in the armed forces. This ensured a continual supply of troops. Military training, like the education system, was another way for the government to further persuade the public to accept its point of view.

Japan used its strengthened military to raise its status in the world. By asserting itself militarily, Japan stood to gain respect and new territory. In 1894, Japan and China went to war over who would control Korea. Japan had always been especially concerned about Korea because it is the closest part of mainland Asia to Japan. When Japan won the war, China lost control of Korea, and Japan gained control of Taiwan.

In 1904, Japan surprised the West by attacking Russian forces over control of Manchuria and matters related to Korea. That conflict ended in 1905 with a Japanese victory and a subsequent rise in patriotic feelings.

By this time, State Shinto and imperialism were firmly linked together. As Japan acquired colonies, it instituted State Shinto as their official religion. Shinto shrines dedicated to Japanese kami were built in Japan's new territories. Shinto priests accompanied Japanese troops to these colonies. Colonists, many of them Buddhist, were made to worship at these shrines to Japanese deities.

In 1912, the Emperor Meiji died, and Crown Prince Yoshihito became Japan's new emperor. This began the Taisho era. During this time, Japan continued to build its military and expand its territory.

At the start of World War I in 1914, Japan saw an opportunity to enlarge its sphere of influence. At the time, Germany was a major power in China, Japan's nearby rival. Japan joined the Allied powers, which included Great Britain, France, and Russia, against the Central powers, which included Germany and Austria-Hungary. Although Japan played a relatively small role in the war, it leveraged its position to strip Germany of its holdings in China. Japan received control of other territory in China as well as Caroline Island, the Mariana, and Marshall Islands in the Pacific Ocean.

Emperor Yoshihito died in 1926. His successor, Hirohito, would usher in yet another period of extraordinary change.

An official portrait of Emperor Showa (Hirohito) wearing his coronation kimono. The coronation took place on November 10, 1928.

The Changing Role of Shrines

The role of Shinto shrines was adjusted to serve the needs of the state. All shrines were ranked in importance, with Ise being the primary shrine. All citizens were to register as parishioners of their local shrine. Having allegiance to a shrine was cast as an integral part of being Japanese.

In the 1800s, the government promoted special shrines to honor those who had died in war. Chief among these was

Emperor Hirohito

Emperor Yoshihito's son, Hirohito, succeeded his father to the imperial throne. Hirohito was born in Japan in 1901, and as a student, developed a keen interest in marine biology, about which he would become an expert. In 1921, he toured Europe, becoming the first Japanese crown prince to visit the West. He developed a fondness for European foods and was particularly impressed by the time he spent with King George V of England. He was attracted to the informality of the British royal family.

In 1924, Hirohito married Princess Nagako. The couple went on to have seven children together. Hirohito became emperor in 1926, when he was twenty-five years old.

Contrary to the name of the Showa era (meaning "enlightened peace"), the first decades of Hirohito's rule were fraught with turmoil. The emperor's exact role in the decisions leading up to World War II is still a subject of debate. After the war and Japan's defeat, Hirohito remained emperor, but his status was reduced. He ruled until his death in 1989.

the Yasukuni Shrine, built in 1869 to honor those who had died to end shogun rule. The dead from subsequent wars would also be buried there. Being enshrined at Yasukuni was considered a great honor. Enshrinement there meant that one's soul was now considered part of the nation.

One war widow noted that after a local mayor paid tribute to her dead husband, her household's standing rose from that of "mere poor peasants [to] … the fine house of a hero, the house of the military nation, upon which the honor of the Japanese people shines. … I must never allow such an honored household to die out."[26]

The Yasukuni Shrine was more than just a place to worship the war dead. It symbolized the prestige of dying in battle. Emperors Meiji, Taisho, and Hirohito all paid homage to those enshrined at Yasukuni.

Smaller, local shrines and memorials to the war dead grew in number and stature. Many received state support, and all served to promote the idea that death in battle was glorious and honorable. One father who saw his son's name inscribed upon a local war memorial said the following:

> I married very young and for a long time had no children. My wife finally bore a son and died. My son grew up fine and healthy. Then he joined the emperor's forces in the Seinan

War and died a manly death in southern Kyushu in a great battle. I loved my son. When I heard that he had died for the emperor, I cried with joy, because for my warrior son there could be no finer death. My son was buried on a mountaintop near Kumamoto. I went there to care for the grave. My son's name was carved on a war memorial for those from Izumo who had fallen for the emperor's sake. I felt glad when I saw my son's name there. I talked with him and felt that he was again walking by my side beneath a great pine tree.[27]

Another shrine of great symbolic importance was the Meiji Shrine. Emperor Meiji ruled for forty-five years and was revered by many. After he died in 1912, there was a popular movement to build a lasting monument to his greatness.

Nationalism and Religious Freedom

Due to pressure from the West, the Meiji Constitution of 1889 included some guarantees of religious freedom. Article Twenty-Eight of the constitution stated that Japanese subjects would "enjoy freedom of religious belief" as long as it did not threaten "peace and order" and did not interfere with "their duties as subjects."[28]

This meant that citizens had the right to practice the religion of their choosing. It could not, however, interfere with the duties required of them by the government. This rule presented a conflict that would occur often as Shinto and the state became ever more entangled. Helen Hardacre writes of the status of Shinto in the constitution, "[there was] a growing tendency to separate it [the constitution] from the sphere of religion and to align it instead with custom and patriotism."[29]

Traditional Japanese drum ceremonies are a popular feature at the Yasukuni Shrine.

The meaning of Shinto was clearly evolving. Those who did not subscribe to State Shinto were viewed suspiciously. Shinto religious groups that were outside the mainstream were suppressed, as were other religions.

Christianity had long been considered a threat to government authority. As the rise of State Shinto linked Shinto and nationalism, the patriotism of Japanese Christians was called into question. One such case involved a Christian school-teacher named Uchimura Kanzo. Uchimura refused to bow to the emperor's signature on the Imperial Rescript on Education to acknowledge its sacred nature. Uchimura tells what happened next:

> After the address of the [principal] and reading of the [Imperial Rescript on Education], the professors and students were asked to go up to the platform one by one, and bow to the imperial signature affixed to the [rescript], in the manner as we used to bow before our ancestral relics prescribed in Buddhist and Shinto ceremonies. I was not at all prepared [for] such a strange ceremony, for [it] was the new invention of the [principal] of the school. … Hesitating in doubt, I took a safer course for my Christian conscience, and in the august presence of sixty professors (all non-Christians, the two other Christian professors beside myself having absented themselves) and over one thousand students, I took my stand

and did not bow. … For a week after the ceremony, I received several students and [professors] who came to me, and with all the meekness I could muster … I told them also that the good Emperor must have given the [rescript] to his subjects not to be bowed unto, but to be obeyed in our daily walks in life.[30]

This incident was reported widely. It was held up as an example of why Christianity and Japanese ethics did not complement one another. Uchimura was fired from his job.

As Japan became more militaristic and nationalistic, the government tolerated dissent, or opposition, less and less. Misgivings about foreign influences such as Christianity grew more extreme. Hardacre notes, "In 1932 … national outrage followed when Christian students from Sophia University refused to pay tribute at the Yasukuni Shrine. Their refusal to bow before the national shrine for the war dead confirmed suspicions that Christians were unpatriotic and Christianity incompatible with Japanese sensibilities."[31]

Shinto and Nationalism

While its involvement in World War I had led to expansion of its empire, Japan still had problems to overcome. The Treaty of Versailles, which officially ended the war, failed to include a racial equality clause sought by the Japanese. This created bad feelings in Japan toward the West in general and the

Dedicated to the memory of Emperor Meiji and Empress Shoken, the Meiji Shrine was officially opened on November 1, 1920.

United States in particular. Negative feelings grew with the passage of the Japanese Exclusion Act, a new anti-immigration law adopted by the United States.

On other fronts, the economy was bleak, and the success of the Bolshevik Revolution in Russia was seen as a threat to the region. In the 1930s, domestic terrorism, political assassinations, and even an attempt on Emperor Hirohito's life created a climate of fear in Japan. All this contributed to conservative ultranationalists demanding a Showa Restoration. This was a call to halt democratic reforms in Japan in favor of imperial and military rule.

As with the Meiji Restoration, Shinto was a factor in this desire. Racist and nationalist elements began to flourish openly in Japan. These attitudes grew from the common belief that, because of its unique history, Japan was superior to all other nations. This idea further led some to think Japan was meant to conquer and rule foreign lands. Shinto beliefs played a prominent part in this thinking. As one scholar wrote,

> People all over the world refer to Japan as the Land of the Gods and call us the descendants of the gods. Indeed, it is exactly as they say. Our country, as a special mark of favor from the heavenly gods, was begotten [created] by them. There is thus so immense a difference between Japan and all the other countries of the world as to defy comparison. We, down to the most humble man and woman, are the descendants of the

gods. Nevertheless ... many people ... do not understand why Japan is the Land of the Gods and we their descendants. ... Japanese ... are superior to the peoples of China, India, Russia, Holland, Siam, Cambodia, and all other countries of the world."[32]

A Dangerous Idea

A popular slogan during the 1930s was *hakko ichiu*, meaning "eight corners of the world" or "all the world under one roof." It refers to the belief that Japan, because of its natural superiority, was justified in its imperialist policies: the invasion and control of other lands. The extension of this logic was that the Japanese Shinto emperor-god should rightfully rule the entire world. This form of patriotism drew upon State Shinto and Confucian ethical ideals. Foreigners were looked down upon as racially, culturally, and morally inferior.

These beliefs were a major factor in Japan's involvement in World War II. As it conquered territory in Asia, the Japanese military forced conquered peoples to work on behalf of the Japanese war effort by building roads or securing natural resources. Because Japan viewed non-Japanese people as inferior, it allowed and sometimes encouraged brutal treatment of non-Japanese.

The belief in Japanese superiority fed other beliefs as well: that the Japanese

A Sacred Place

The Meiji Shrine is one of the holiest sites in Japan. Construction of the shrine began in 1915 in Tokyo, in a garden often visited by Emperor Meiji and his wife, Empress Shoken. Costs and labor factors connected to World War I slowed construction. However, in an exceptional development, common citizens from all over Japan donated money and labor to complete the shrine. The grounds were planted with 120,000 donated trees of 365 different species. This outpouring from citizens testified to the importance of the emperor and of Shinto. After the shrine was completed in 1920, a ceremony was performed to enshrine the souls of Emperor Meiji and Empress Shoken, who had died in 1914.

Much of the original shrine complex was destroyed during World War II, but it was rebuilt by 1958. The shrine has two main parts: Naien is the inner precinct and garden. It contains shrine buildings, including the treasure museum, housing items belonging to the emperor and empress. Gaien is the outer area and garden. This section includes a picture gallery and eighty large murals depicting events from the lives of the emperor and empress. The national sports stadium of Japan is located on the grounds.

were invincible and that there was no greater sacrifice than to give one's life for the emperor. One Japanese veteran of World War II recounted in later years how he and others of his generation viewed their duty toward Japan and their sense of those they fought:

We students never really argued about the war [being right] among ourselves. Since Meiji times, Japan had been advancing in that direction. In order to enrich the nation, Japan had to strengthen the army. Population increased, so to increase the nation's productive capacities, the country had to expand. [It was] for the sake of the development of the race. Japan was not the only nation that expanded aggressively. When we were ready to graduate from school in 1942, we thought, "Let's go!" I, who was studying history, look back now and recognize that was only one way to view things. But at that time we all looked and said, "Japan must take this course." Today, were my child to say, "I want to enter the military," I would reply, "Don't do it!" But at that time we didn't have that kind of choice.

Those days were full of hostility and hatred toward the enemy. We didn't know much about America. They were simply "the enemy." It didn't occur to us that behind the enemy there were governments, people, Christians, anything. We just thought, "they are here, we must fight them." We had no knowledge of how America was founded. What races made up America. Nothing. We saw them as lower animals.[33]

Many factors contributed to Japan's decision to attack the United States in 1941. Much of the ideology, or beliefs, behind Japan's extreme nationalism can be tied to the history of State Shinto. The education system and mandatory military service promoted the idea that the first loyalty of Japanese citizens was to the state. The emperor, according to State Shinto, was the godlike leader of the state.

Shrines encouraged the idea that dying in battle for the emperor was the most noble and desirable death possible. An atmosphere of economic uncertainty and a perception of unfair treatment by the West made many Japanese feel that war with Europe and North America was inevitable. A half century of military successes abroad led many to believe that Japan would be victorious. This, combined with certainty in the rightness of their beliefs, provided part of Japan's motivation for entering World War II. Ultimately, though, State Shinto's fate would forever be linked to the war and its outcome.

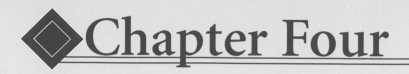

Chapter Four

Shinto and Changes in Government

The years leading up to and during World War II marked the peak of State Shinto's influence. The philosophies associated with the national religion helped propel Japan toward war and gave its citizens motivation to sacrifice and fight. Japan's defeat in the war, however, signified the collapse of State Shinto.

This change had huge implications. The status of the emperor was reduced, and a new constitution officially separated the state from religion. This constitution also emphasized freedom of religion in a new way for Japan. Shinto lost its official status, but it continued to be a strong force in Japan. State Shinto collapsed, but Shinto became expressed in other ways that showed connection to the government. Perhaps the most notable example of this was the controversy over the Yasukuni Shrine.

The Emperor at War's End

Although the Japanese met with much success early in the war, they could not sustain it. On July 26, 1945, the leaders of the United States, Great Britain, and China announced the Potsdam Declaration. This called for the unconditional surrender of the Japanese. The stated alternative was "prompt and utter destruction."[34]

Japan did not submit, and the United States detonated an atomic bomb over Hiroshima on August 6 and Nagasaki on August 9. On August 15, Emperor Hirohito, afraid that all of Japan would be destroyed, made a radio broadcast to the nation. This marked the first time that his voice was heard by the nation. In this historic broadcast, Hirohito asked that the Japanese people concede, or give in, to the Allies "by enduring the unendurable and suffering what is insufferable."[35]

The Children's Peace Monument

The Peace Memorial Park was built in Hiroshima to recall the dropping of the atomic bomb over the city in 1945 and to promote a more peaceful world. The Peace Memorial Museum is located in the park. Using artifacts, words, and pictures, the museum explains how the bomb devastated the city.

The park houses many memorials to the victims of the bomb. The Children's Peace Monument is dedicated to a girl named Sadako Sasaki and other children who perished. Sadako became very ill because of radiation from the bombing. She hoped to cure herself by folding a thousand origami cranes, an act that was said to bring good luck. Sadako died before finishing the cranes. A statue of a girl holding a huge folded crane is part of the Children's Peace Monument. Children from all over the world still fold cranes and send them to the park, where they are displayed.

The city of Hiroshima holds a Peace Memorial Ceremony on the 6th of August every year to commemorate the victims of the atomic bomb.

Some historians have speculated that if the emperor had not made his request, the Japanese military might have fought on, resulting in the Allies' total destruction of Japan. Instead, on September 2, the Instrument of Surrender was signed on the deck of the USS *Missouri*. The war was over.

At the urging of U.S. General Douglas MacArthur, Emperor Hirohito released

A Japanese woman prays at a Shinto shrine among the ruins of her home in December, 1944.

a document on New Year's Day, 1946. In this message, Hirohito shocked many Japanese by professing his humanity. He stated that he was not a living god and that the imperial line was not divine. He announced that the power of the state could not be based on "the false [idea] that the emperor is divine or that the Japanese people are superior to other races."[36] These statements directly contradicted the philosophy of the Meiji Constitution and specific declarations made by State Shinto. By renouncing that he was divine, the emperor took an important step toward weakening State Shinto.

The divinity of the emperor had been a subject of much debate among the Allied forces. Many believed he deserved to be tried as a war criminal. Indeed, Hirohito volunteered to be held responsible for Japan's actions. In his memoirs, MacArthur recalls Hirohito's words and his own reaction to them:

> "I come to you, General MacArthur, to offer myself to the judgment of the powers you represent as the one to bear sole responsibility for every political and military decision made and action taken by my people in the conduct of war," [Hirohito said]. A tremendous impression swept me. This courageous assumption of a responsibility … moved me to the very marrow of my bones. He was an emperor by inherent birth, but in that instant I knew I faced the First Gentleman of Japan in his own right.[37]

MacArthur realized that the postwar transition would be easier if the emperor remained in office, though in a diminished capacity. In a memo to the U.S. War Department, he wrote that prosecuting Hirohito for war crimes would "unquestionably cause a tremendous convulsion among the Japanese people. … He is a symbol which unites all Japanese. Destroy him and the nation will disintegrate."[38]

The decision was made not to arrest Hirohito. Instead, he stayed on and served in a symbolic way while MacArthur took charge of the country's affairs.

The People Gain Power

The emperor remained, but much else changed during the Allied occupation of Japan that lasted from the end of the war in 1945 until 1952. Some of these changes were listed in the new constitution of 1947.

The writing of the constitution was controversial. Japanese and American scholars and lawyers had different ideas about what it should include. The Japanese commission recommended conservative changes to the Meiji Constitution of 1889. MacArthur found this unacceptable and ordered his staff to write an entirely new constitution, which they did. They then presented it to the Japanese. A few changes were made, but in effect, the American-written document became the new constitution of Japan in 1947.

Technically, the new constitution was an amendment to the Meiji Constitution. In reality, however, it provided for an entirely different sort of government, based on different principles. This is clear from the start of the preamble:

> We, the Japanese people, acting through our duly elected representatives in the National Diet (the

U.S. General Douglas MacArthur and Emperor Hirohito met for the first time on September 27, 1945.

elected legislature), determined that we shall secure for ourselves and our posterity the fruits of peaceful cooperation with all nations and the blessings of liberty throughout this land, and resolved that never again shall we be visited with the horrors of war through the action of government, do proclaim that sovereign power resides with the people and do firmly establish this Constitution. Government is a sacred trust of the people, the authority for which is derived from the people, the powers of which are exercised by the representatives of the people, and the benefits of which are enjoyed by the people.[39]

In the new order, all political power in Japan originated from the people, acting through their elected representatives. This is fundamentally different from the Meiji Constitution, which declared the emperor, by virtue of his divine lineage, to be the center of power. The first chapter of the constitution and subsequent articles reinforce this new point. They specify that the emperor's function is symbolic only, and that he has no governmental power. In the new government, the Diet would establish laws and be the highest branch of government.

What Would an Emperor Do?

With the emperor's ruling authority abolished, the constitution had to address the

The closing session of the Lower House of the Diet on August 8, 2005. The Diet is Japan's legislature.

Emperor Hirohito, in civilian clothes, visits with children in Chira, Japan in 1946.

question of what sort of service the emperor would perform. Articles 6 and 7 spelled it out. Article 6 allowed the emperor to appoint the prime minister, as designated by the Diet, and to appoint the chief judge of the supreme court, as designated by the cabinet.

Article 7 gave the emperor the responsibilities of promoting the constitution, laws, cabinet orders, and treaties. He could open and close legislative sessions.

He also could announce the appointment of newly elected members of the Diet and the dismissals of other officials. His main function was to act as a proponent for government policy and protocol. He would award honors, entertain foreign dignitaries, and perform ceremonial functions.

The new constitution was clear—the emperor's powers were purely symbolic, and he could only act in an official

Tenrikyo

A woman named Nakayama Miki founded the religion of Tenrikyo, which means "Religion of Divine Wisdom." Based on Shinto, Tenrikyo has become the largest and most successful of Japan's new religions.

In 1838, Nakayama had a religious revelation while she and her family were undergoing ritual treatments for pain. She believed she had been possessed by a god known as the Lord of Divine Wisdom. Out of this experience, she developed the religious doctrines that form Tenrikyo.

Nakayama believed that "God the Parent" wanted her to be the "Shrine of God" and mediate between God and humans. Her followers knew her as Oyasama, or "Honored Mother." She taught that people should live a joyous life for 115 years. She believed this to be a natural lifespan. Charity, selflessness, and optimism were central to this goal.

Tenrikyo grew to include more than two million followers, most of whom live in Japan. To serve its followers and spread its beliefs, Tenrikyo runs a radio station, a university, and a library.

Perhaps the most notable example of this has been revealed at Yasukuni shrine.

Since the conflicts that led to the Meiji Restoration, Japan has enshrined at Yasukuni the souls of about 2.5 million Japanese war dead. Weapons and military memorabilia are also housed at the shrine. Emperors and officials often visited the shrine during the era of State Shinto. The creed of State Shinto taught that it was a glorious honor to die in war and be venerated at Yasukuni. Far more than just a war memorial, Yasukuni shrine is where the war dead are most visibly worshipped. Because the shrine made obvious the overlap of state ideals and Shinto practices, it became a controversial place.

Debate about Yasukuni grew heated in the late 1970s, when fourteen Class

A convicted war criminals from World War II were enshrined there. Many people remembered Japanese brutality toward the non-Japanese who were conquered or captured during the war. To those who suffered at the hands of the Japanese, enshrining war criminals felt like an insult. They claimed the Japanese government was attempting to rewrite history. Calls to remove the war criminals, especially former prime minister General Tojo Hideki, failed repeatedly.

Prime Ministers' Visits Raise Eyebrows

While some Japanese continue to view the shrine as a monument to imperialism and

Prime Minister Koizumi Junichiro attends a ceremony at Yasukuni Shrine marking the 61st anniversary of Japan's surrender on August 15, 2006.

war, others see it as a symbol of patriotism. Still others say they visit the shrine only to remember the war and to pray for peace. Prime Minister Koizumi Junichiro, who was prime minister from 2001 to 2006, made several trips to Yasukuni to the concern of former Japanese colonies.

Koizumi's successor, Abe Shinzo, has been unable to escape this issue, especially when he travels abroad. During a trip to China in 2006, Abe was asked to talk about potential tensions between the two countries because of a report that he had visited Yasukuni. He replied,

In the meetings today, Chinese leaders referred to the spirit of using history as a mirror to progress toward the future. They also mentioned that they would like political obstacles to be removed. In response, I said we shall look at past history squarely and shall continue to conduct [ourselves] as a peaceful nation. Japan has come through the sixty years of the postwar period on the basis of the deep remorse ... that [we] ... caused tremendous damage and suffering to the people of the Asian countries, and left scars in those people. This feeling is shared by the ... people who have lived these sixty years and is a feeling that I also share. This feeling will not change in the future.

With regard to the visits to Yasukuni shrine, I explained my thoughts. Whether I have visited or will visit Yasukuni shrine is not something I shall make clear since this is a matter that has been turned into a diplomatic and political issue. I shall not elaborate on it. That said, from the viewpoint that both sides shall overcome political difficulties and promote the sound development of the two countries, I shall address this matter appropriately.[42]

Abe tried to obscure the issue by refusing to disclose his stance on visiting the shrine. Abe did visit Yasukuni in April

Abe Shinzo became Japan's youngest prime minister since World War II on September 26, 2006.

2007, about six months after he made his statement in China. Predictably, the visit generated much interest at home and abroad. One newspaper said the prime minister reportedly made an offering at the shrine of a potted plant worth 50,000 yen, which had come out of his own pocket.

The newspaper questioned why Abe made the offering when "China and South Korea have repeatedly lodged against Japanese prime ministers' visits to the controversial shrine."[43] Abe was not the first to do this, however. According to the same newspaper article, his predecessor, Prime Minister Koizumi, had angered China, South Korea, and other countries with his repeated visits to Yasukuni.

People debated whether these shrine visits by government officials violate the constitutional clauses pertaining to the separation of religion and state. Some officials have said their visits were made as private citizens, not as state employees. Writer Helen Hardacre said this about distinguishing between a prime minister's shrine visits being a function of his private life or his public role:

> From roughly 1972 to the present, Diet members and the media have questioned every prime minister in order to clarify this distinction and the government's intentions. Did the prime minister use a private or a public car in traveling to the shrine? Did he make an offering to the shrine from his private or public funds? Did he sign the shrine registry with his personal name, or did he add his official title?[44]

In the case of Prime Minister Abe's visit to the shrine, Hardacre's questions receive mixed answers. Abe signed in at the shrine using his official title of prime minister. He bought his offering of a plant with his own money, however, and reportedly paid for the trip himself.

As for the imperial family, Hirohito used to visit the shrine but stopped because of his displeasure over the en-shrinement of the war criminals. Imperial envoys now appear at festivals there bearing offerings from the emperor.

More Concerns Arise

Most of the visitors to Yasukuni are private citizens. According to Kiyama Terumichi in the book *Japan at War*, an official from the shrine said this about the visitors:

> We have eight million worshippers annually. I can probably classify them into three types. First are the mere sightseers. Then there are the war comrades and the bereaved families. Naturally, each year, membership in their associations has been dwindling. Then there is a third group, those who come here in search of some meaning. There are many in that category that feel we have to appreciate the war dead because they perished for the sake of the nation. To convey that message to history, to enshrine the war dead here, means to them an assurance of the resurrection of the Japanese mind and spirit. They feel they must do that. People who have been thinking like that … come here. Their numbers have gradually been increasing.[45]

The way of thinking that the priest referred to frightens many in Japan and abroad. They worry that the third type of visitor may be distorting Japan's war history or promoting denial of Japanese war

During the Autumn Festival in 2004, shrine priests presented offerings and read the Gosaimon, *or Imperial message, to the deities at Tokyo's Yasukuni Shrine.*

guilt. Further concern has been raised because Yasukuni has become a meeting place for ultranationalist groups.

Some Japanese have tried to formally reestablish state support for Yasukuni. Proposed legislation authorizing this action was defeated several times on the basis that it violated the constitution. Hardacre writes, "Whether in the form of financial support or formal tribute by the cabinet, the Self-Defense Force, [or] the emperor, state patronage of the Yasukuni Shrine inevitably gives the appearance of state sanction of the shrine, its history, and its traditions."[46] The issue is likely to continue to be debated.

The relationship between the Japan-ese government and Shinto changed radically in the aftermath of World War II. A new constitution separated the state and religion and underscored freedom of religion. While State Shinto disappeared, Shinto itself continued to be linked to the government. Debates over the symbolism and role of Yasukuni Shrine attest to this.

The emperor remains an important symbol, too, no longer as a deity but rather as an emblem of the common ancestry of the Japanese. Part of what makes one Japanese is not simply citizenship, but a sense of descent from seemingly endless generations of Japanese who have gone before.

Chapter Five

Shinto in Daily Life

Although most Japanese do not identify themselves as religious, aspects of Shinto remain important parts of daily life in Japan. Shinto represents a feature of Japanese culture that is considered unique. Because of this, Shinto is a symbolic unifying agent for Japanese people.

Shinto is expressed in modern life in several different ways. Shared Japanese ethics are based on deep-rooted Shinto principles, which also draw from Buddhism and Confucianism. Many Japanese people practice Shinto and Buddhist rituals on a regular basis. Additionally, Shinto festivals are a highly visible part of Japanese culture.

Good Behavior

The concept of wa is essential to Shinto. *Wa* means "benign (harmless) harmony."

According to Shinto, it is important to maintain wa in all relations with people and nature. The way to preserve one's wa is to follow the norms and rules of society. According to Shinto, disorder will result in society and the natural world if people do not follow these standards. Thus, following social codes of conduct and getting along with others is of great consequence for society. These traits have been part of Japanese culture for thousands of years.

Japanese mythology portrayed gods who experienced human feelings such as love, anger, and kindness. Those who behaved well and had good relations with others achieved favors and rewards. Those who did not were punished. In mythology, harming others or behaving badly met with negative consequences, such as being cast out of the community.

All societies have laws and generally understood codes of conduct to maintain order. Japanese people teach their children from an early age to highly value human relationships. They learn that a happy and satisfying life comes from being personally connected to others. Children are led to understand that they play a role in their family, school, and community, and that everyone else does too.

The Japanese view of society can be compared to an enormous and beautiful spider web. Each strand of the web represents an individual, and each is dependent on the others to keep the web's form and function. This state of interconnected dependence is considered natural and good. It becomes a burden only if too many social obligations overwhelm it.

As part of this interdependence, the Shinto ethic emphasizes conformity. If one does not conform to convention, he risks losing face and bringing shame on himself and his extended household. This extended household can include one's family, ancestral spirits, school, workplace, or other group. If embarrassment does occur, there are socially approved ways to make things right. For example, one might bow deeply or give a gift to the person one has offended. Sometimes a whole group of people is disrupted by the action—or perhaps inaction—on the part of another group. In such a situation, the offending group is expected to repair the

The Significance of Bowing

Japanese people bow often and for many reasons. Shinto and Buddhist rituals require bowing to show respect. Everyday interactions between people also call for frequent bowing. For example, Japanese people typically bow instead of shaking hands when greeting each other. Circumstances such as social rank and age dictate how deeply one bows. The person of lesser status and age is supposed to bow deeper and longer than the person of greater sta-tus and age. Bowing is also a means of being polite, expressing thanks, asking for a favor, and apologizing. In all of these ways, bowing is symbolic of the values of Japanese society.

Bowing (ojigi) is a social gesture of greeting used instead of a handshake.

damage. Historian C. Scott Littleton gives an example from everyday life:

> [W]hen Japan's famous Shinkansen "Bullet Train" is late, every employee from the engineer to the conductor, hostesses, and ticket sellers feels responsible and will apologize profusely to delayed passengers. Once atonement is made, the shame ceases and the burden it imposes is lifted.[47]

Wa in Everyday Life

Wa is important to Japanese views on nature and purity as well. Since all of Japan is considered sacred space, pollution is seen as affecting both the environment and spiritual life. Those responsible for the upkeep of Shinto shrines have often become active in local environmental causes.

Shinto addresses issues of personal purity. The Shinto obsession with wa is reflected in a variety of Japanese customs that, at first glance, might not seem religious, such as removing one's shoes before entering a house and taking a daily bath. Both customs are, essentially, expressions not only of purification—the interior of a home is, after all, a "sacred space" compared to the outside world—but of the maintenance of a harmonious balance in the world, as well.

Other religions and philosophies that have mingled with Shinto reinforce its ethics, or codes of conduct. According to Buddhism, the ultimate goal of life is to cease to be reborn by reaching the enlightened state of nirvana. To achieve this, one must accumulate positive karma. The path to nirvana involves subduing one's own desires. This complements the Shinto belief that individuals must not give in to selfish tendencies.

Confucius's teachings also contribute to Japanese social ethics and wa. His writings emphasize caring for others, even at the expense of oneself. On the subject of perfect virtue, Confucius stated his version of the golden rule:

> It is ... to behave to everyone as if you were receiving a great guest. To employ the people as if you were assisting at a great sacrifice. To not to do to others as you would not wish done to yourself. To have no murmuring against you in the country, and none in the family.[48]

This, too, reaffirms the philosophy of wa. Confucius believed that self-restraint and consideration for others are valuable traits. These values are widespread in Japan today.

Ritual and Practice

Modern Japan does not view itself as a religious nation. Normally, between 60 and 80 percent of Japanese people describe themselves as "not religious." The overwhelming majority of Japanese people, however, do participate in religious practices or rituals.

Both Shinto and Buddhism are more about practice than belief. In Shinto, people do not need to believe in kami to participate in Shinto rituals with sincerity. Performing the ritual correctly is the most important thing. The faith or belief behind the ritual is secondary.

More than 80 percent of Japanese take part in Shinto rituals. Almost as many participate in Buddhist practices. This means that many people engage in both Shinto and Buddhist rituals. Participating in religious rituals, however, does not necessarily mean one is agreeing to a particular set of beliefs. It simply reflects that one is sharing in the common culture, or even just practicing being Japanese.

There are many different kinds of rituals. Some are marked by national holidays. Some are performed at home at a kamidana or Buddha altar, while others are observed at shrines or temples. Many of them mark special events in a person's life.

Rites of Passage

One common Shinto practice is *hatsumiyamairi*, which is a baby's first visit to a shrine. This usually occurs on the thirty-second day after birth for a boy and the thirty-third day for a girl. At the shrine, the baby becomes an official member of the parish. He or she is then considered to be under the protection of that shrine's kami.

The festival of Shichigosan, better known as the 7-5-3 festival, represents another childhood ritual. Parents and their children visit their parish shrine to give thanks to kami and to pray for a bright future. Boys go when they are three years old and again at age five; girls visit when they are three and seven.

Childhood is officially ended on Seijin Shiki (Adult's Day). This is a national holiday celebrating young adults. The age of legal adulthood is age twenty in Japan. Traditionally, those who have recently turned or will soon become twenty years old dress in adult clothing. Women wear a kimono (a long robe) and men wear a suit. They visit a shrine to give thanks.

Weddings and Funerals

In the past, most Japanese couples married in a Shinto wedding ceremony. Now fewer than 20 percent of Japanese use only Shinto rites for weddings. These weddings are typically small affairs, which only close family members attend. The bride's traditional dress is a white kimono and scarf. The groom wears a kimono as well. Shinto weddings include a ritual to purify the couple, prayers, and a traditional dance performance.

Most weddings are no longer held at Shinto shrines. Instead, hotels and wedding halls have become popular venues. Other Western trappings that are now commonly part of Japanese weddings are bridal gowns, cakes, wedding rings, and honeymoons. As they do through-

It is customary for young girls attending their shichi-go-san ceremony to carry a bag of chitose-ame, a candy that symbolizes health and longevity.

A June bride and her groom sail to their wedding procession, while a boat of family members follows.

out their lives, Japanese people often choose to mix and match Shinto, Buddhist, and Christian traditions in their weddings. A typical combination of religious traditions occurring over the life of an individual is illustrated in the following story.

Bundled in colorful silks, the newborn Keiko Shirato was taken by her parents to a neighborhood Shinto shrine, where a white-gowned priest pronounced blessings for a long and healthy life. On three childhood birthdays she also visited Shinto shrines, clapping her hands and clanging bells to awaken the gods so she could pray to them. In 1980, Keiko used Buddhist omens to select a [lucky] wedding day. But she exchanged Christian vows with her fiancé in a small chapel at one of Tokyo's elegant hotels. Keiko, now 26 and a mother, expects that some day her ashes will be [buried] in a Buddhist cemetery, where her descendants will annually return with a Buddhist priest to pray in her honor.

To Keiko, [mixing different] religious [practices] is perfectly natural. "I owe respect to my ancestors and show it through Buddhism," she explains. "I'm a Japanese, so I do all the little Shinto rituals. And I thought a Christian marriage would be real pretty."[49]

In Japan, most funerals and memorial services are performed in the Buddhist tradition. Shinto views death as impure, and it does not dwell on the afterlife. Though Shinto funerals and cemeteries do exist, they are uncommon, and their rituals are largely derived from Buddhist traditions.

Most Japanese are happy with combining a little from one religion and a little from another. In fact, they even have a name for this practice, calling it *chuto-hanpa*. After all, even ancient Shinto blended Buddhism and Confucianism.

Holidays and Festivals

Two categories of holidays are observed in Japan. *Matsuri* are festivals derived from Shinto. *Nencho gyo* are annual events that are usually connected to Buddhism. Some of these are national holidays, but many are not. Some observances are large in scale, while others are small. They are held throughout the year all over Japan.

Matsuri have many different purposes, including asking kami for a good rice harvest or preventing natural disasters. Some matsuri have attracted many tourists. Their main purpose, however, is to emphasize the public display of historical continuity. Celebrations reinforce the ties that bind together members of the community and help to establish community identity.

A holiday that the Japanese celebrate with great enthusiasm is Shogatsu Matsuri, a three-day New Year's festival held from January 1 to January 3. To prepare for the fresh start that the new year represents, people clean their houses and finish up business projects. Families gather to relax, watch special television programs, and put the old year behind them. Houses are decorated and special foods, such as *ozoni* (a type of soup) and *mochi* (pounded rice cakes), are served. According to Littleton, "the most important activity of Shogatsu Matsuri is a visit to a shrine or temple to make an offering and pray for prosperity and good health in the coming months. In some sects, miniature household shrines and the tablets bearing the names of family ancestors are ritually burned and replaced with new ones."[50]

Gift Giving

Giving a gift in Japan is more than just a nice thing to do; it is a ritualized way of expressing respect and friendship. Japanese values are expressed in certain customs related to gift giving and gift receiving. Gifts are typically exchanged in midsummer and at the end of the year, as well as for happy occasions, such as birthdays, weddings, and graduations. Giving gifts to business associates is a common practice. When people return from a vacation, they are expected to hand out small gifts from the trip.

The receiver of a gift returns a thank-you gift to the giver that is typically half the value of the original gift. Gifts are always wrapped. They are presented and accepted with both hands, and each person bows. The giver de-emphasizes the gift's value by saying, "This is just a small thing." These customs are meant to demonstrate that gifts themselves are not as important as the relationship between the giver and receiver.

On New Year's Eve, many Buddhist temples ring their bells 108 times to rid humanity of the 108 types of earthly desires that cause suffering. On New Year's Day, millions of Japanese visit shrines to ask for blessings from the kami. The day is supposed to be an especially lucky one to make such requests.

Another widely observed Japanese holiday is Obon. This is a Buddhist festival celebrated in the summer to commemorate deceased ancestors. Ancestral graves are cleaned, as the spirits of one's ancestors are expected to visit. Many people visit Buddhist temples on this day to pray and make offerings of food, flowers, or incense. *Bon odori*, a type of dance, is a typical feature of the celebration. Some people put up lanterns near their houses to guide the spirits of the departed home.

At the festival's end, these lanterns are placed into rivers to guide the spirits back to their realm.

Japanese people often visit gravesites and celebrate ancestors on the first days of the spring and autumn equinoxes. These are the two days of the year when there are twelve hours of daylight and twelve hours of night.

An especially colorful festival is Tanabata (Star Festival). This is always celebrated on the seventh day of the seventh month of the year. Because some people still use the lunar calendar to date this festival, it is celebrated in July in some parts of the country and in August in other areas. According to Chinese legend, this is the day when two particular stars that are usually separated by the Milky Way are able to meet. A tradition is to write wishes on colored pieces of paper and tie them to a bamboo tree placed near the home. Some communities sponsor large parades with dancing and fireworks.

One of Japan's most famous festivals is the Gion festival in the ancient city of Kyoto. This celebration dates from the year 869, when an epidemic swept through Kyoto. People went to the Yasaka Shrine and prayed to Gozu Tenno, the god of good health, to end their suffering. They erected sixty-six tall spears symbolizing the sixty-six provinces of Japan. Soon, the sickness subsided, and Gozu Tenno was praised. A festival was held in his honor.

Today's Gion festival recalls these events and is held through the month of July. A highlight of the festivities is the parade of floats. Some of the floats are massive, standing two stories high and weighing 10 tons (9t). Hundreds of thousands of people come to view the parade.

All in the Family

Some festivals honor certain members of the family. Examples include the national holidays of Children's Day (also called Boy's Festival) and Respect for the Aged Day. Hina, known as Girl's Festival or Doll's Festival, is held in the spring. Families with young daughters celebrate in hopes of giving the girls a fortunate future.

Ceremonial dolls that belonged to previous generations are central to the tradition. The dolls, dressed in fancy, traditional Japanese costumes, are carefully

Festive lanterns are a common feature of the Gion matsuri festival, held each July in Kyoto, Japan.

set on display for several days, sometimes with well-crafted, miniature furniture and accessories. New dolls may be bought by the girl's parents or given to her by others as a gift. Peach blossoms, which signify the feminine traits of gentility, composure, and tranquility, are used as decorations.

An especially fortunate girl will have

The Hina Matsuri, or Doll Festival, is held on March 3rd each year. More than 1,500 of these "hina" dolls will be sent to sea to pray for the health of their former owners.

a set of well-dressed emperor and empress dolls, along with members of their court. These dolls are displayed on special little steps for one day only.

The Hina festival originated in China with paper dolls. In an effort to get rid of their problems, people would gather on March 3rd and write down their concerns on paper dolls. Then they took the dolls to a river and tossed them in. The day coincided with the beginning of spring and symbolized a casting off of old misfortunes.

Children's Day began as an ancient celebration of a family's boys. On the fifth day of the fifth month, families who have boys fly carp-shaped streamers outside their house. In Japanese culture, the carp represents strength and success. Dolls of famous warriors and other heroes are displayed inside the house, as well, to commemorate strength and success.

National events celebrating children are held, too, as part of Children's Day. These include a kids' olympics and a variety of kids' theater performances.

Neighbors Celebrate

Most communities consider their local festivals to be very important. These matsuri celebrate the local kami. Some of the activities take place at the local shrine, while others occur in the wider commu-

Golden Week

Along with the New Year and Obon, Golden Week is one of three major holiday celebrations in Japan. Four national holidays occur in Japan during this one week in spring, and many of the people take vacations during this time.

Golden Week begins with Showa Day on April 29th. This date observes the birthday of the late Emperor Hirohito. May 3rd is Constitution Day and celebrates the anniversary of the constitution of 1947. Greenery Day is marked on May 4th and honors nature and the environment. May 5th is Children's Day, otherwise known as Boy's Festival. On this day, families pray for the health and success of their sons.

nity. For a larger gathering, a mikoshi, or portable shrine, is paraded through the area, bestowing blessings on the neighborhood. Typically, three local groups represent the community at these festivals: the merchants' association, the neighborhood residents' association, and the shrine elders' association.

Others play a role in the festivities too. Children carry a mini mikoshi around the neighborhood. With exuberant cries, young men and women carry the real mikoshi down the street. Singers and drummers parade along with them, and priests chant, pray, and purify the shrine. At day's end, entertainers provide a more relaxed atmosphere. One community festival is colorfully described by author Kawano Satsuki:

On the second day of the festival, younger self-employed men ... organize a children's show and a lottery. Just as the ritual procession expels misfortune and illness from the neighborhood, so the children's show involves the act of defending the neighborhood from evil influences. A monster Mummy Man— similar to a Frankenstein—arrives from another planet and begins destroying buildings in Sakae's business area. When children failed to repel the monster by throwing paper balls, Ultraman (similar to Superman) appears in the dark sky and flies down to save the neighborhood—a doll comes sliding down a rope—by beating the monster until he apologizes.[51]

Kawano notes that the festival's formal rituals and the children's entertainment have a common theme. The acts of worshipping kami and defending against a pretend monster aim to guarantee the safety of Sakae's residents and bind the neighborhood together.

The annual Danjiri Matsuri passes through the town of Kishiwada in Osaka, Japan.

Like Shinto's ethics and rituals, festivals are woven into Japanese culture. Although most contemporary Japanese people do not think of themselves as religious, typical Japanese life includes many aspects of religion. To mark events in the cycle of life or to protect their communities, Japanese often turn to Shinto traditions. People participate in these because they are believers, or they hope for benefits, or they feel obliged. Sometimes they share in the traditions just because they are part of the Japanese way. Members of society form ties and affirm their community identity through aspects of Shinto. This religion, hand in hand with Buddhism and Confucianism, continues to be an important way of approaching the world and living one's life with concern for one and all.

Notes

Chapter 1: The Japanese Way

1. Quoted in Ian Reader and George J. Tanabe Jr., *Practically Religious: Worldly Benefits and the Common Religion of Japan* (Honolulu: University of Hawaii Press, 1998), 113.
2. T. R. Reid, *Confucius Lives Next Door* (New York: Random House, 1999), 171.
3. Ibid.
4. Ibid., 89–90.
5. Kakuzo Okakura, *The Book of Tea* (New York: Dover Publications, Inc., 1964), http://www.gutenberg.org/catalog/world/readfile?fk_files=37599&pageno=2/ (accessed April 12, 2007).
6. Quoted in Rhoads Murphey, *East Asia: A New History* (New York: Longman, 2001), 194.
7. Susan Orlean, "Transcendence," in *Travelers' Tales: Japan,* ed. Donald W. George and Amy Greimann Carlson (Palo Alto, CA: Travelers' Tales, 1999), 129.
8. C. Scott Littleton, *Understanding Shinto* (London: Duncan Baird, 2002), 75.
9. Reader and Tanabe, *Practically Religious,* 260.
10. Noriko S. Nomura, *I Am Shinto* (New York: The Rosen Publishing Group, Inc., 1996), 13.
11. Brandon Toropov and Luke Buckles O.P., "Purity in Shinto," *Religion and Ethics – Shinto,* http://www.bbc.co.uk/religion/religions/shinto/beliefs/purity.shtml (accessed March 8, 2007).

Chapter 2: Shinto Helps Unite Japan

12. Helen Hardacre, *Shinto and the State 1868–1988* (Princeton, NJ: Princeton University Press, 1989), 16.
13. W. G. Ashton, trans., "Nihongi," *Sacred Texts Archive,* http://www.sacred-texts.com/shi/nihon0.htm (accessed April 16, 2007).
14. "The Meiji Restoration and Modernization," *Contemporary Japan: A Teaching Workbook* (Columbia University, East Asian Curriculum Project), http://afe.easia.columbia.edu/japan/japanworkbook/modernhist/meiji.html (accessed April 16, 2007).
15. Hardacre, *Shinto and the State 1868–1988,* 19.
16. Quoted in "Meiji Restoration and Modernization."

17. Ibid.
18. Namiko Abe, "Japanese National Anthem," *Your Guide to Japanese Language*, http://japanese.about.com/library/weekly/aa030400.htm (accessed April 16, 2007).
19. Hardacre, *Shinto and the State 1868–1988*, 28.
20. Quoted in James Edward Ketelaar, *Of Heretics and Martyrs in Meiji Japan* (Princeton, NJ: Princeton University Press, 1990), 77.
21. Richard Hooker, "Chinese Philosophy: Confucius," *World Civilizations*, http://www.wsu.edu/~dee/CHPHIL/CONF.HTM (accessed April 9, 2007).
22. Hardacre, *Shinto and the State 1868–1988*, 44.
23. Ibid., 44–45.
24. Ibid., 45.

Chapter 3: Shinto and the Second World War

25. "Imperial Rescript on Education," Meiji Shrine (Meiji Jingu), http://www.meijijingu.or.jp/english/intro/education/index.htm (accessed April 30, 2007).
26. Quoted in Hardacre, *Shinto and the State 1868–1988*, 92.
27. Ibid., 92–93.
28. "Meiji Restoration and Modernization."
29. Hardacre, *Shinto and the State 1868–1988*, 120.
30. Quoted in Hardacre, *Shinto and the State 1868–1988*, 123.
31. Hardacre, *Shinto and the State 1868–1988*, 25.
32. Quoted in Littleton, *Understanding Shinto*, 34.
33. Quoted in Haruko Taya Cook and Theodore F. Cook, *Japan at War: An Oral History* (New York: The New Press, 1992), 451–452.

Chapter 4: Shinto and Changes in Government

34. "Potsdam Declaration," *Birth of the Constitution of Japan* (Tokyo: National Diet Library, 2003–2004), http://www.ndl.go.jp/constitution/e/etc/c06.html (accessed May 6, 2007).
35. Quoted in "Japan: World War II and the Occupation, 1941–1952," *Library of Congress Country Study: Japan*, http://lcweb2.loc.gov/cgibin/query/r?frd/cstdy:@field(DOCID+jp0046 (accessed May 6, 2007).
36. Quoted in "Japan: The Status of the Emperor," *Library of Congress Country Study: Japan*, http://lcweb2.loc.gov/cgi-bin/query/r?frd/cstdy:@field(DOCID+jp0204 (accessed May 6, 2007).
37. Quoted in "Emperor Hirohito," www.spartacus.schoolnet.co.uk/2WWhirohito.htm (accessed May 4, 2007).
38. "Incoming Classified Message from: CINCAFPAC Adv Tokyo, Japan To: War Department," *Birth of the Constitution of Japan* (Tokyo:

National Diet Library, 2003–2004), http://www.ndl.go.jp/constitution/e/shiryo/03/064/064_001r.html (accessed May 7, 2007).

39. The Constitution of Japan, http://www.kantei.go.jp/foreign/constitution_and_government_of_japan/constitution_e.html (accessed May 7, 2007).

40. Ibid.

41. Quoted in Hardacre, *Shinto and the State 1868–1988*, 137.

42. "Press Conference by Prime Minister Shinzo Abe Following His Visit to China (October 8, 2006)," Speeches and Statements by Prime Minister, http://www.kantei.go.jp/foreign/abespeech/2006/10/08chinapress_e.html (accessed May 9, 2007).

43. "Abe made offering to Yasukuni Shrine in late April," *Japan Today*, May 8, 2007, http://www.japantoday.com/jp/news/406011 (accessed May 9, 2007).

44. Hardacre, *Shinto and the State 1868–1988*, 144.

45. Quoted in Cook, *Japan at War*, 453.

46. Hardacre, *Shinto and the State 1868–1988*, 147.

Chapter 5: Shinto in Daily Life

47. Littleton, *Understanding Shinto*, 59.

48. James Legge, trans., "Confucian Analects," *Sacred Texts Archive*, http://www.sacred-texts.com/cfu/conf1.htm (accessed May 14, 2007).

49. "Religious Attitudes Today," *Contemporary Japan: A Teaching Workbook* (New York: Columbia University East Asian Curriculum Project, 2004), http://afe.easia.columbia.edu/japan/japanworkbook/religion/reltod.html (accessed May 14, 2007).

50. Littleton, *Understanding Shinto*, 80.

51. Satsuki Kawano, *Ritual Practice in Modern Japan* (Honolulu: University of Hawai'i Press, 2005), 100.

For Further Reading

Books

John Carroll and Michael Yamashita. *Japan: Soul of a Nation*. North Clarendon, VT: Tuttle Publishing, 2003. This book combines text and color photos to bring alive Japan's geographic and cultural environment.

Bruce Feiler. *Learning to Bow: Inside the Heart of Japan*. New York: Harper Perennial, 2004. The author recounts his experiences as a junior high school teacher in Japan. He describes his encounters with Japanese cultural characteristics such as group loyalty and community responsibility.

Paula Hartz. *Shinto*. New York: Facts on File, 2004. This book covers the basics of Shinto, including its origins, belief system, rituals, and festivals.

Helen and William McAlpine. *Tales from Japan*. New York: Oxford University Press, 2002. A collection of Japanese legends and fairy tales, this book includes the story of the creation of Japan and stories of various kami, including the sea spirit and the moon god.

Shozo Sato. *Tea Ceremony*. North Clarendon, VT: Tuttle Publishing, 2005. This book walks kids of all ages through the basic steps of the Japanese tea ceremony.

Paul D. Storie. *Amaterasu: Return of the Sun, A Japanese Myth*. Minneapolis: Graphic Universe, 2007. This graphic novel retells traditional Japanese myths about Amaterasu, the Japanese sun goddess.

Robert Whiting. *You Gotta Have Wa*. New York: Vintage, 1990. This book examines how the Japanese concept of *wa*, or group harmony, affects the game of baseball. The author focuses on American baseball players who have played in Japan, comparing their experiences in Japan with their experiences in United States baseball leagues.

Internet Sources

Ishii Kenji. "Annual Events and the Transformation of Japanese Religious Life." Institute for Japanese Culture and Classics, Kokugakuin University, 1994, 1997. http://www2.kokugakuin.ac.jp/ijcc/wp/cpjr/folkbeliefs/ishii.html. Kenji discusses annual events of the Japanese calendar. He includes the results of several surveys given to Japanese people.

Kids Web Japan. "Paying Your Respects to the Seven Deities of Good Fortune." http://web-japan.org/kidsweb/explore/calendar/january/shichifukujin.html.

This Web site describes the Seven Deities of Good Fortune (Shichifuku-jin), as well as their history.

Shinto Online Network Association. "Shinto." http://jinja.jp/english/s-0.html. This Web site provides a description of Shinto. Details about the four types of Shinto are included.

Alice N. Yamada. "Shinto: The Way of the Gods." http://www.trincoll.edu/zines/tj/tj4.4.96/articles/cover.html. Yamada describes Shinto shrines and how Shinto relates to the Japanese way of life.

Works Consulted

Books

Michael Ashkenazi. *Matsuri: Festivals of a Japanese Town*. Honolulu: University of Hawaii Press, 1993. The rituals and festivals of a small town in Japan are surveyed in this work. The relationships of festivals to religion, culture, and location are analyzed.

W. G. Beasley. *The Japanese Experience: A Short History of Japan*. Berkeley: University of California Press, 1999. The author delivers an overview of the history of Japan from its distant past to the postwar period. Several helpful maps are included.

Elizabeth Breuilly, Joanne O'Brien, and Martin Palmer. *Religions of the World*. New York: Facts On File, Inc., 1997. This is a brief survey of the major religions of the world. It contains an overview of the beliefs and practices of Shinto and Buddhism.

Haruko Taya Cook and Theodore F. Cook. *Japan at War: An Oral History*. New York: The New Press, 1992. Japanese survivors of World War II from different walks of life give their personal histories and views on the war. The authors provide commentary.

John Dower. *Embracing Defeat: Japan in the Wake of World War II*. New York: W.W. Norton and Co., 1999. Dower describes the transformation of Japan from a war-torn and exhausted country to a democratic world power. This book contains interesting anecdotes about evolving views of the emperor after the war.

Donald W. George and Amy Greimann Carlson, ed. *Travelers' Tales: Japan*. Palo Alto, CA: Travelers' Tales, 1999. This book is an anthology of accounts by Western travelers and residents in Japan. Many aspects of Japanese culture and society are examined through different points of view.

Helen Hardacre. *Shinto and the State 1868–1988*. Princeton, NJ: Princeton University Press, 1989. Hardacre's book provides a detailed account of the relations between religion and government in Japan from 1868–1988. The roles of both historical figures and common citizens in church/state issues are carefully considered.

Satsuki Kawano. *Ritual Practice in Modern Japan*. Honolulu: University of Hawaii Press, 2005. The author studies one particular city to examine the role of festivals and rituals in modern life. Traditional practices are researched and explained.

James Edward Ketelaar. *Of Heretics and Martyrs in Meiji Japan: Buddhism and Its Persecution*. Princeton, NJ: Princeton

University Press, 1990. This work focuses on Buddhists during the Meiji period. The persecution and ultimate survival of Japanese Buddhists are investigated.

C. Scott Littleton. *Understanding Shinto.* London: Duncan Baird, 2002. Littleton provides an excellent introduction to Shinto. Many themes are discussed, including the history, texts, principles, beliefs, and place in society of Shinto.

Rhoads Murphey. *East Asia: A New History.* New York: Addison-Wesley Educational Publishers Inc., 2001. This work provides a broad overview of the history of East Asia, from prehistory to the twentieth century. The main focus is on China and Japan.

John K. Nelson. *Enduring Identities: The Guise of Shinto in Contemporary Japan.* Honolulu: University of Hawaii Press, 2000. Nelson cites examples of the many ways in which Shinto is relevant to contemporary society. He discusses the many ways in which religion is a key aspect of the identity of Japanese people.

Noriko S. Nomura. *I Am Shinto.* New York: The Rosen Publishing Group, Inc., 1996. This is a work of children's literature. A Japanese American girl living in Hawaii learns about and explains the basics of Shinto beliefs and practices.

Ian Reader and George J. Tanabe Jr. *Practically Religious: Worldly Benefits and the Common Religion of Japan.* Honolulu: University of Hawaii Press, 1998. Reader and Tanabe discuss the nature of prayer in Japan. The roots and contemporary practices of religion are studied and interpreted.

T. R. Reid. *Confucius Lives Next Door.* New York: Random House, 1999. This is a sometimes humorous look at life for an American living in Japan. Reid compares the culture and values of the East and West.

Scott Schnell. *The Rousing Drum: Ritual Practice in a Japanese Community.* Honolulu: University of Hawaii Press, 1999. Schnell examines a particular drum ritual and places it in a larger context. Far from being simply religious, this ritual had political and economic meanings as well.

John W. Traphagan. *The Practice of Concern: Ritual, Well-Being, and Aging in Rural Japan.* Durham, North Carolina: Carolina Academic Press, 2004. The author studies northern Japanese ideas about aging and ritual. Traphagan shows connections between religion and health in Japan.

Periodicals

"Abe made offering to Yasukuni Shrine in late April." *Japan Today,* May 8, 2007, http://www.japantoday.com/jp/news/406011 (accessed May 9, 2007).

"Hirohito quit Yasukuni Shrine visits over concerns about war criminals." *International Herald Tribune,* April 26, 2007, http://www.iht.com/articles/2007/04/26/news/japan.php (accessed May 8, 2007).

Internet Sources

W. G. Ashton, trans. "Nihongi." *Sacred Texts Archive.* http://www.sacred-texts.com/shi/nihon0.htm (accessed April 16, 2007).

Ayako and Steven Archer. "Gift Giving." *A Beginner's Guide to Japan.* http://www.traveltst.ca/japan_guide/99-japa/abj23-e.htm (accessed May 16, 2007).

Rosemarie Bernard. "Shinto and Ecology: Practice and Orientations to Nature." *Introduction to Shinto.* http://environment.harvard.edu/religion/religion/shinto/index.html (accessed March 2, 1007).

Birth of the Constitution of Japan. Tokyo: National Diet Library, 2003–2004. http://www.ndl.go.jp/constitution/e/index.html (accessed May 7, 2007, et al.)

"Bodh Gaya, India." *Places of Peace and Power.* http://www.sacredsites.com/asia/india/buddhist.html (accessed April 10, 2007).

"Bowing." *Japan-Guide.com.* http://www.japan-guide.com/e/ e2000.html (accessed May 16, 2007).

"Chanoyu and religion." *The Tradition of Chanoyu.* http://www.omotesenke.jp/english/chanoyu/2_3_4.html (accessed April 10, 2007).

Confucianism and the Chinese Scholastic System. http://www.csupomona.edu/~plin/ls201/confucian2.html (accessed May 4, 2007).

"Confucius." *Stanford Encyclopedia of Philosophy.* http://plato.stanford.edu/entries/confucius/#ConEdu (accessed May 14, 2007).

The Constitution of Japan. http://www.kantei.go.jp/foreign/constitution_and_government_of_japan/constitution_e.html (accessed May 7, 2007).

A Country Study: Japan. Washington, D.C.: The Library of Congress, 2005. http://lcweb2.loc.gov/frd/cs/jptoc.html (accessed April 9, 2007, et al.)

Embassy of Japan in the United States of America. "Matsuri: The Festivals of Japan." http://www.us.emb-japan.go.jp/jicc/spotfestivals.htm (accessed May 16, 2007).

Emperor Hirohito. www.spartacus.schoolnet.co.uk/2WWhirohito.htm (accessed May 4, 2007).

"Festivals." *Japan-Guide.com.* http://www.japan-guide.com/e/e2063.html (accessed May 15, 2007).

Hina Matsuri: Doll Festival. http://www.ginkoya.com/pages/girlsday.html (accessed May 15, 2007).

Richard Hooker. "Chinese Philosophy: Confucius." *World Civilizations.* 1996. http://www.wsu.edu/~dee/CHPHIL/CONF.HTM (accessed April 9, 2007).

"Japan City Guides: Hiroshima Peace Park & Peace Memorial Museum." *Japan Visitor.* http://www.japanvisitor.com/index.php?cID=357&pID=1303 (accessed May 10, 2007).

"Japan PM visits Yasukuni shrine." BBC News, October 17, 2005. http://news.bbc.co.uk/2/hi/asia-pacific/4348280.stm (accessed May 8, 2007).

Japan Society. "Gion Festival." *Journey Through Japan.* http://journey.japansociety.org/culture/culture_detail.cfm?

id_news=54484446&type=1& search_keywords=a (accessed May 16, 2007).

Japan Society. "Hiroshima Peace Park." *Journey Through Japan.* http://www. journeythroughjapan.org/culture/ culture_detail.cfm?id_news=59281352 (accessed May 10, 2007).

Japanese National Holidays, Year 2007. http://www.asahi-net.or.jp/~tc9w -ball/useful/holiday.htm (accessed May 15, 2007).

Kakuzo Okakura. *The Book of Tea.* New York: Dover Publications, Inc., 1964. http://www.gutenberg.org/catalog/wor ld/readfile?fk_files=37599 &pageno= 2/ (accessed April 12, 2007).

James Legge, trans. "Confucian Analects." *Sacred Texts Archives.* http://www .sacred-texts.com/cfu/conf1.htm (accessed May 14, 2007).

Meiji Jingu http://www.meijijingu.or.jp /english/index.htm (accessed April 30, 2007).

"The Meiji Restoration and Moderniza- tion." *Contemporary Japan: A Teaching Workbook.* New York: Columbia Uni- versity East Asian Curriculum Project, 2004. http://afe.easia.columbia.edu/ japan/japanworkbook/modernhist/me iji.html (accessed April 16, 2007).

Namiko Abe. "Japanese National Anthem." *Your Guide to Japanese Lan- guage.* http://japanese.about.com /library/weekly/aa030400.htm (accessed April 16, 2007).

"Press Conference by Prime Minister Shinzo Abe Following His Visit to China (October 8, 2006)." Speeches and Statements by Prime Minister. http://www.kantei.go.jp/foreign/ abespeech/2006/10/08chinapress_e.ht ml (accessed May 9, 2007).

Religion and Ethics–Shinto. http://www .bbc.co.uk/religion/religions/shinto/ (accessed March 8, 2007, et al.).

"Religious Attitudes Today." *Contempo- rary Japan: A Teaching Workbook.* New York: Columbia University East Asian Curriculum Project, 2004. http://afe .easia.columbia.edu/japan/japan workbook/religion/reltod.html (accessed May 14, 2007).

"Sacred Spaces in Shinto." *Teaching Com- parative Religion Through Art and Architecture.* http://ias.berkeley.edu /orias/visuals/japan_visuals/shinto.HTM (accessed March 2, 2007).

"Shinto." *JapanZone.* http://www.japan -zone.com/omnibus/shinto.shtml (accessed March 2, 2007).

"Shinto." *Overview of World Religions Pro- ject.* http://philtar.ucsm.ac.uk/ encyclopedia/shinto/index.html (accessed April 16, 2007).

"Shinto Shrines." *Japan-Guide.com.* http://www.japan-guide.com/e /e2059.html (accessed March 2, 2007).

Shizuko Mishima. "Bowing in Japan." *Japan for Visitors.* http://gojapan.about. com/cs/etiquetteinjapan/a/bowing.ht m (accessed May 16, 2007).

Shizuko Mishima. "Japanese End of Year Gift Giving." *Japan for Visitors.* http:// gojapan.about.com/cs/tradition custom/a/oseibo.htm (accessed May 14, 2007).

"Shrine at Ise, Japan." *Sacred Places.*

http://witcombe.sbc.edu/sacredplaces /ise.html (accessed March 11, 2007).

"Tenrikyo." *The Religious Movements Homepage Project.* Charlottesville, VA: University of Virginia, 2005. http: //religiousmovements.lib.virginia.edu /nrms/tenrikyo.html (accessed May 9, 2007).

"Time Tested Relations." *Trends in Japan,* July 8, 2003, http://web-japan.org /trends/arts/art030708.html (accessed April 16, 2007).

Waka Poetry http://www.reiki.fi/english /reiki/history/poetry/waka1.htm (accessed April 16, 2007).

N. Alice Yamada. "Shinto: The Way of the Gods." *Trincoll Journal,* 1996. http:// www.trincoll.edu/zines/tj/tj4.4.96/arti-cles/cover.html (accessed March 2, 2007).

Index

Picture Credits

About the Author

Suzanne Sonnier holds a master's degree in history and is a former high school and university instructor. She writes and lives near Chicago, Illinois.

About the Consultant

Dr. John Traphagan is director of the Center for East Asian Studies at the University of Texas, Austin.